Objective-C 2.0 Essentials

Third Edition

Objective-C 2.0 Essentials – Third Edition

ISBN-13: 978-1480262102

Find more eBooks online at *http://www.eBookFrenzy.com*.

Rev. 3.1

Table of Contents

1. About Objective-C Essentials

1.1 Why are you reading this?

On the surface this sounds like an odd opening sentence for a programming book. After all, if this were a book about JavaScript or PHP it would be safe to assume that you planned to develop some kind of web site or web application. Similarly, if this were a Visual Basic book it would be a good bet that you had plans to write a Windows application. Indeed, had this question been asked a few years ago, it could have been guessed with a reasonable level of confidence that you wanted to learn Objective-C in order to develop some software to run on Apple's Mac OS X operating system. Now, however, there is a greater likelihood that you plan to develop an application to run on the iPhone or iPad.

The iPhone and the iPad, after all, run a special version of Mac OS X called iOS. Given that Objective-C is the programming language of choice for this operating system it should come as no surprise that before you can develop iOS applications you first need to learn how to program in Objective-C.

Fully updated for Modern Objective-C syntax, the objective of this book is to teach the skills necessary to program in Objective-C using a style that is easy to follow, rich in examples and accessible to those who have never used Objective-C before. Topics covered include the fundamentals of Objective-C such as variables, looping and flow control. Also included are details of object-oriented programming, working with files and memory and the Objective-C Foundation framework.

Those who have developed using other programming languages such as C, C++, C# or Java will find much about Objective-C that is familiar. That said, there are aspects of the language syntax that are unique to Objective-C. Even experienced programmers should therefore expect to spend some time transitioning to this increasingly popular programming language before embarking on a major development project.

Whatever your background and experience, we have worked hard to make this book as useful and helpful as possible as you traverse the Objective-C learning curve.

1.2 **Supported Platforms**

After all this talk about Mac OS X and iOS, it is important to note that Objective-C is not confined to Apple's operating systems. In fact, Objective-C is available on a wide range of platforms including Linux, NetBSD, OpenBSD, FreeBSD, Solaris and Windows in the form of the open source *GNUstep* environment. This means that anyone with access to a GNUstep supported platform can learn Objective-C, though if your ultimate objective is to develop for iOS or Mac OS X, you will at some point need access to an Intel based Mac computer system.

Perhaps one key advantage to using a Mac OS X system for learning Objective-C comes in the form of access to Apple's Xcode development environment. Another benefit of learning Objective-C on a Mac OS X system is that as new features are added to the language, those improvements are typically made available on Mac OS X before they make it onto other operating system platforms. That being said, other than references to Xcode in early chapters, the remainder of this book is intended to be as platform agnostic as possible.

2. The History of Objective-C

Before learning the intricacies of a new programming language it is often worth taking a little time to learn about the history and legacy of that language. In this chapter of *Objective-C 2.0 Essentials* we will provide a brief overview of the origins of Objective-C and the business history that ultimately led to it becoming the programming language of choice for both Mac OS X and iOS.

2.1 The C Programming Language

Objective-C is based on a programming language called, quite simply, *C*. The origins of the C programming language can be traced back nearly 40 years to two engineers named Dennis Ritchie and Ken Thompson working at what is now known as AT&T Bell Labs. At the time, the two were working on developing the UNIX operating system on PDP-7 and PDP-11 systems. After attempts to write this operating system using assembly language (essentially using sequences of instruction codes understood by the processor), it was decided that a higher level, more programmer friendly programming language was required to handle the complexity of an operating system such as UNIX. The first attempt was a language called *B*. The *B* language, which was based on a language called *BCPL*, was found to be lacking. Taking the next initial from the *BCPL* name, the *C* language was created and subsequently used to write much of the UNIX operating system kernel and infrastructure. As far as we can tell, *C* was so successful that new languages named *P* and *L* never needed to be created.

2.2 The Smalltalk programming Language

The C programming language is what is known as a *procedural* language. As such, this means that it lacks features such as object oriented programming. Object oriented programming advocates the creation of small, clearly defined code objects that can be assembled and reused to create more complex systems.

3

An early attempt at an object-oriented programming language was developed by a team including Alan Kay (who later went to work for Apple) and Dan Ingalls at Xerox PARC (Palo Alto Research Center) in the 1970s. This language is known as Smalltalk.

2.3 C meets Smalltalk

An interesting history lesson so far, but what does this have to with Objective-C? Well, in the 1980s, two developers named Brad Cox and Tom Love extended the C programming language to support the object oriented features of Smalltalk. This melding of languages ultimately culminated in the creation of Objective-C. Objective-C was subsequently adopted by the Free Software Foundation and released under the terms of the GNU Public License (GPL).

2.4 Objective-C and Apple

To understand how Objective-C, a language based on two 40 year-old programming languages, ended up being the language of choice on Mac OS X and the latest cutting edge smart phones and tablets from Apple it is necessary to move away from technology for a while and talk about business.

In the 1980s Steve Jobs and Steve Wozniak founded Apple Computer. After many years of success, Steve Jobs hired PepsiCo CEO John Sculley to help take Apple to the next level of business success. To cut a long story short, a boardroom battle ensued and Steve Jobs got pushed out of the company (for the long version of the story pick up a used copy of John Sculley's book *Odyssey: From Pepsi to Apple*) leaving John Sculley in charge.

After leaving Apple, Jobs started a new company called NeXT to design an entirely new generation of computer system. The operating system developed by NeXT to run on these computers was called NeXTstep. In order to develop NeXTstep, NeXT licensed Objective-C. NeXT subsequently joined forces with Sun Microsystems to create a standardized version of NeXTstep named OPENstep which the Free Software Foundation then adopted as GNUstep.

During the 1990s, John Sculley left Apple and a procession of new CEOs came and went. During this time, Apple had been losing market share and struggling to come out with a new operating system to replace the aging Mac OS. After a number of failed attempts and partnerships, it was eventually decided that rather than try to write a new operating system, Apple should acquire a company that already had one. During Gil Amelio's brief reign as CEO, a shortlist of two companies was drawn up. One was a company called Be, Inc. founded by a former Apple employee named Jean-Louis Gassée, and the other was NeXT.

Ultimately, NeXT was selected and Steve Jobs once again joined Apple. In another boardroom struggle (another long story as outlined in Gil Amelio's book *On the Firing Line: My 500 Days at Apple*) Steve Jobs pushed out Gil Amelio and once again became CEO of the company he had founded all those years ago.

The rest, as they say, is history. NeXTStep formed the foundation of what became Mac OS X, bringing with it Objective-C. Mac OS X was subsequently modified to provide the iOS operating system for the spectacularly successful iPhone and iPad devices.

2.5 Modern Objective-C

As the decades passed by, aspects of Objective-C such as some elements of language syntax and memory management began to appear somewhat dated, particularly when compared to more contemporary languages such as Java and C#. In recognition of this fact Objective-C has continued to evolve and, in recent years in particular, a number of additions and improvements have been made to the language to make the task of writing code easier and less error prone for the programmer. These improvements have combined to create what is typically referred to as "Modern Objective-C".

3. Installing Xcode and Compiling Objective-C on Mac OS X

Although Objective-C is available on a range of platforms via the GNUstep environment, if you are planning to develop iOS or Mac OS X applications you are going to need to use an Intel based Mac OS X system at some point in the future.

Perhaps the biggest advantage of using Mac OS X as your Objective-C learning platform (aside from the ability to develop iOS and Mac OS X applications) is the fact that you get to use Apple's Xcode development tool. Xcode is an integrated development environment (IDE) within which you will code, compile, test and debug your iOS and Mac OS X applications.

In this chapter we will cover the steps involved in installing Xcode and writing and compiling a simple Objective-C program in this environment.

3.1 Identifying if you have an Intel or PowerPC based Mac

Only Intel based Mac OS X systems can be used to run the latest versions of Xcode. If you have an older, PowerPC based Mac then you will need to purchase a new system before you can begin your app development project. If you are unsure of the processor type inside your Mac, you can find this information by clicking on the Apple logo in the top left hand corner of the screen and selecting the *About This Mac* option from the menu. In the resulting dialog, check the *Processor* line. Figure 3-1 illustrates the results obtained on an Intel based system.

If the dialog on your Mac does not reflect the presence of an Intel based processor then your current system is, sadly, unsuitable as a platform for running the latest versions of Xcode.

In addition, the current edition of the Xcode environment requires that the version of Mac OS X running on the system be version 10.7.4 or later. If the "About This Mac" dialog does not indicate that Mac OS X 10.7.4 or later is running, click on the *Software Update...* button to download and install the appropriate operating system upgrades.

Figure 3-1

3.2 **Installing the Xcode Development Environment**

The best way to obtain the latest version of the Xcode development environment is to download it from the Apple Developer Center web site at:

https://developer.apple.com/xcode/

The download is over 1.6GB in size and may take a number of hours to complete depending on the speed of your internet connection.

3.3 **Starting Xcode**

Having successfully installed Xcode, the next step is to launch it so that we can write and then run a sample Objective-C application. To start up Xcode, open the Finder and search for *Xcode.app*. Since you will be making frequent use of this tool, take this opportunity to drag and drop it into your dock for easier access in the future. Click on the Xcode icon in the dock to launch the tool.

Once Xcode has loaded, and assuming this is the first time you have used Xcode on this system, you will be presented with the *Welcome* screen from which you are ready to proceed:

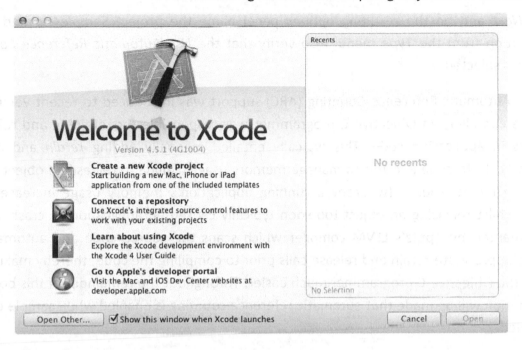

Figure 3-2

Click on the option to *Create a new Xcode project* to display the template selection screen. Within the template selection screen, select the *Application* entry listed beneath *MacOS X* in the left hand panel followed by *Command Line Tool* in the main panel:

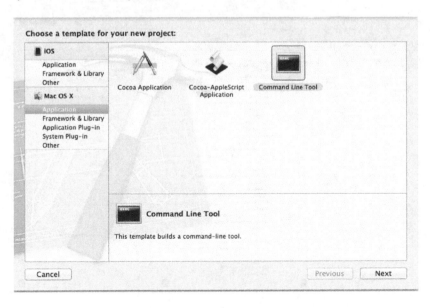

Figure 3-3

Click *Next* and on the resulting options panel name the project *SampleApp* and select *Foundation* from the *Type* menu. Also verify that the *Use Automatic Reference Counting* option is selected.

Before Automatic Reference Counting (ARC) support was introduced to recent versions of Apple's compiler, an Objective-C programmer was responsible for retaining and releasing objects in application code. This typically entailed manually adding *retain* and *release* method calls to code in order to manage memory usage. Failing to release an object would result in memory leaks (whereby a running application's memory usage increases over time), whilst releasing an object too soon typically caused an application to crash. ARC is implemented by Apple's LLVM compiler which scans the source code and automatically inserts appropriate retain and release calls prior to compiling the code, thereby making the life of the Objective-C programmer much easier. Throughout the remainder of this book the assumption will be made that automatic reference counting is enabled when sample code is compiled.

Click *Next* and on the subsequent screen choose a suitable location on the local file system for the project to be created before clicking on the *Create* button.

Xcode will subsequently create the new project and open the main Xcode window:

Figure 3-4

Before proceeding we should take some time to look at what Xcode has done for us. Firstly it has created a group of files that we will need to create our command-line based application. Some of these are Objective-C source code files (with a .m extension) where we will enter the code to make our application work, whilst others are header or interface files (.h) that are included by the source files and are where we will also need to put our own declarations and definitions.

The list of files is displayed in the *Project Navigator* located in the left hand panel of the main Xcode project window. A toolbar at the top of this panel contains tabs to change the information displayed in this panel including options to display debugging information, log history and issues such as compilation warnings and errors. In Figure 3-5, for example, the option has been selected to display the Issues Navigator (which in this case displays some compilation errors):

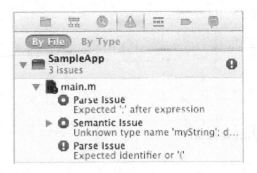

Figure 3-5

By default, the center panel of the window shows the build settings for the application. This includes, amongst other settings, the project identifier specified during the project creation process and the target architecture and operating system (in this case Mac OS X and Intel 64-bit).

In addition to the Build Settings screen, tabs are provided to view and modify additional settings consisting of Build Phases and Build Rules. To return to these panels at any future point in time, make sure the *Project Navigator* is selected in the left hand panel (selected using the folder icon in the toolbar at the top of the panel) and select the top item (the project name) in the navigator list.

When a source file is selected from the list in the navigator panel, the contents of that file will appear in the center panel where it may then be edited. To open the file in a separate editing window, simply double click on the file in the list.

3.4 **Writing an Objective-C Application with Xcode**

As previously outlined, Objective-C source files are identified by the *.m* filename extension. In the case of our example, Xcode has pre-created a main source file named *main.m* and populated it with some basic code ready for us to edit. To view the code, select *main.m* from the list of files located in the Project Navigator so that the code appears in the editor area. The skeleton code reads as follows:

```
#import <Foundation/Foundation.h>

int main(int argc, const char * argv[])
{

    @autoreleasepool {
        // insert code here...
        NSLog(@"Hello, World!");
    }
    return 0;
}
```

Modify the *NSLog* line so that it reads:

```
NSLog(@"This is my first Objective-C App!");
```

With the change made, the next step is to compile and run the application. Since the code is intended to display a message in the console, the first step is to make sure the Xcode console window is displayed by selecting the *View -> Debug Area -> Activate Console* menu option. Next, run the application by selecting the *Run* option located in the Xcode toolbar. Once this option has been selected, Xcode will compile the source code and run the application, displaying the message in the Xcode console panel:

```
All Output ⇕                                          Clear   □  ▥  □
 2012-11-16 10:18:26.314 SampleApp[35525:403] This is my first Objective-C App!
```

3.5 **Compiling Objective-C from the Command Line**

While Xcode provides a powerful environment that will prove invaluable for larger scale projects, for compiling and running such a simple application as the one we have been working with in this chapter it is a little bit of overkill. It is also a fact that some developers feel that development environments like Xcode just get in the way and prefer to use a basic editor and command line tools to develop applications. After all, in the days before integrated development environments came into favor, this was how all applications were developed.

Whilst we are not suggesting that everyone abandon Xcode in favor of the *vi* editor and GNU compiler, it is useful to know that the option to work from the command line is available.

Before attempting to compile code from the command line, the first step is to ensure that the Xcode *Command Line Tools* are installed. To achieve this, select the *Xcode -> Preferences* menu option and in the preferences dialog, select the *Downloads* category. If the Command Line Tools are not yet installed, click on the *Install* button to begin the installation process.

Using your favorite text or programming editor, create a file named *hello.m* containing the following Objective-C code:

```
#import <Foundation/Foundation.h>

int main(int argc, const char * argv[])
{
    @autoreleasepool {
        // insert code here...
        NSLog(@"Hello, World!");
    }
    return 0;
}
```

Save the file and then open a Terminal window (if you aren't already working in one), change directory to the folder containing the source file and compile the application with the following command:

```
clang -fobjc-arc -framework Foundation hello.m -o hello
```

This instructs the clang *compiler front end* to initiate the compilation of the source code located in *hello.m* and output the resulting executable binary to a file named *hello*. The clang tool is referred to as a compiler "front end" because it does not perform that actual compilation work. Instead it calls a *back end* compiler to perform the compilation work. In the case of Objective-C, this role is filled by the LLVM compiler.

The *–framework* directive (also referred to as a *build flag* or *compilation option*) instructs the compiler to include the Foundation framework in the compilation process. It is this framework on which all Objective-C applications are built. Failure to include this directive will result in compilation errors relating to undefined symbols.

Finally, the *–fobjc_arc* option instructs the compiler to use automatic reference counting (ARC).

Assuming the code compiles without error it can be run as follows:

```
./hello
2012-04-18 13:27:11.621 hello[275:707] Hello, World!
```

Compared to using Xcode that seems much simpler, but keep in mind that the power of Xcode really becomes evident when you start developing larger scale projects. In addition, Xcode includes a powerful user interface design tool called Interface Builder that will be essential when developing either iOS apps or Mac OS X applications that require a graphical user interface.

3.6 **Summary**

The goal of this chapter has been to outline the steps involved in installing the Xcode development environment on Mac OS X. Objective-C programs can be written and compiled both from within Xcode and via the command prompt in a Terminal window. A brief overview of memory management and Automatic Reference Counting has been provided followed by the creation, compilation and execution of a simple Objective-C program.

4. Objective-C 2.0 Data Types

When we look at the different types of software that run on computer systems, from financial applications to graphics intensive games, it is easy to forget that computers are really just binary machines. Binary systems work in terms of 0 and 1, true or false, set and unset. All the data sitting in RAM, stored on disk drives and flowing through circuit boards and buses are nothing more than sequences of 1s and 0s. Each 1 or 0 is referred to as a *bit* and bits are grouped together in blocks of 8, each group being referred to as a *byte*. When people talk about 32-bit and 64-bit computer systems they are talking about the number of bits that can be handled simultaneously by the CPU bus. A 64-bit CPU, for example, is able to handle data in 64-bit blocks, resulting in faster performance than a 32-bit based system.

Humans, of course, don't think in binary. We work with decimal numbers, letters and words. In order for a human to easily (easily being a relative term in this context) program a computer, some middle ground between human and computer thinking is needed. This is where programming languages such as Objective-C come into play. Programming languages allow humans to express instructions to a computer in terms and structures we understand, and then compile it down to a format that can be executed by a computer.

One of the fundamentals of any program involves data, and programming languages such as Objective-C define a set of *data types* that allow us to work with data in a format we understand when writing a computer program. For example, if we want to store a number in an Objective-C program we could do so with syntax similar to the following:

```
int mynumber = 10;
```

In the above example, we have created a variable named *mynumber* of data type *integer* by using the keyword *int*. We then assigned the value of 10 to this variable. Once we know that *int* means we are specifying a variable of integer data type we have an understanding of what is happening in this particular line of an Objective-C program. When we compile the source code down to the machine code used by the CPU, the number 10 is seen by the computer in binary as:

```
1010
```

Similarly, we can express a letter, the visual representation of a digit ('0' through to '9') or punctuation mark (referred to in computer terminology as *characters*) using the following syntax:

```
char myletter = 'c';
```

Once again, this is understandable by a human programmer, but gets compiled down to a binary sequence for the CPU to understand. In this case, the letter 'c' is represented by the decimal number 99 using the ASCII table (an internationally recognized standard that assigns numeric values to human readable characters). When converted to binary, it is stored as:

```
1100011
```

Now that we have a basic understanding of the concept of data types and why they are necessary we can take a closer look at the different data types and qualifiers supported by Objective-C.

4.1 **int Data Type**

The Objective-C *int* data type can store a positive or negative whole number (in other words a number with no decimal places). The actual size or range of integer that can be handled by the *int* data type is machine and compiler implementation dependent. Typically the amount of storage allocated to int values is either 32-bit or 64-bit depending on the implementation of Objective-C on that platform or the CPU on which the compiler is running. It is important to note, however, that the operating system also plays a role in whether int values are 32 or 64-bit. For example the CPU in a computer may be 64-bit but the operating system running on it may only be 32-bit.

For example, on a 32-bit implementation, the maximum range of an unsigned *int* is 0 to 4294967295. On a 64-bit system this range would be 0 to 18,446,744,073,709,551,615. When dealing with *signed int* values, the ranges are −2,147,483,648 to +2,147,483,647 and

–9,223,372,036,854,775,808 to +9,223,372,036,854,775,807 for 32-bit and 64-bit implementations respectively.

When writing an Objective-C program, the only guarantee you have is that an int will be *at least* 32-bits wide. To avoid future problems when compiling the code on other platforms it is safer to limit int values to the 32-bit range, rather than assume that 64-bit will be available.

By default, int values are decimal (i.e. based on number base 10). To express an int in Octal (number base 8) simply precede the number with a zero (0). For example:

```
int myoctal = 024;
```

Similarly, an int may be expressed in number base 16 (hexadecimal) by preceding the number with *0x*, for example:

```
int myhex = 0xFFA2;
```

4.2 char Data Type

The Objective-C char data type is used to store a single character such as a letter, numerical digit or punctuation mark or space character. For example, the following lines assign a variety of different characters to char type variables:

```
char myChar = 'w';
char myChar = '2';
char myChar = ':';
```

4.2.1 Special Characters/Escape Sequences

In addition to the standard set of characters outlined above, there is also a range of *special characters* (also referred to as *escape sequences*) available for specifying items such as a new line or tab. These special characters are identified by prefixing the character with a backslash (a concept referred to as *escaping*). For example, the following assigns a new line to the variable named newline:

```
char newline = '\n';
```

In essence, any character that is preceded by a backslash is considered to be a special character and is treated accordingly. This raises the question as to what to do if you actually want a backslash character. This is achieved by *escaping* the backslash itself:

```
char myslash = '\\'; Assign a backslash to a variable
```

Commonly used special characters supported by Objective-C are as follows:

\a - Sound alert
\b - Backspace
\f - Form feed
\n - New line
\r - Carriage return
\t - Horizontal tab
\v - Vertical tab
\\ - Backslash
\" - Double quote (used when placing a double quote into a string declaration)
\' - Single quote (used when placing a single quote into a string declaration)

4.3 **float Data Type**

The Objective-C *float* data type is used to store *floating point* values, in other words values containing decimal places. For example, 456.12 would be stored in a *float* data type. In practice, all floating point values are stored as a different data type (called *double*) by default. We will be covering the *double* data type next, but if you specifically want to use a *float* data type, you must append an *f* onto the end of the value. For example:

```
float myfloat = 123.432f
```

For convenience when working with exceptionally large numbers, both floating point and double data type values can be specified using scientific notation (also known as standard form or exponential notation). For example, we can express 67.7×10^4 in Objective-C as:

```
float myfloat = 67.7e4
```

4.4 **double Data Type**

The Objective-C *double* data type is used to store larger values than can be handled by the *float* data type. The term *double* comes from the fact that a *double* can handle values twice the size of a *float*. As previously mentioned, all floating point values are stored as double data types unless the value is followed by an 'f' to specifically specify a float rather than as a double.

4.5 **id Data Type**

As we will see in later chapters of this book, Objective-C is an object oriented language. As such much of the way a program will be structured is in the form of reusable objects. These objects are called upon to perform tasks and return results. Often, the information passed into an object and the results returned will be in the form of yet another object. The *id* data type is a general purpose data type that can be used to store a reference to any object, regardless of its type.

4.6 **BOOL Data Type**

Objective-C, like other languages, includes a data type for the purpose of handling true or false (1 or 0) conditions. Such a data type is declared using either the *_Bool* or *BOOL* keywords (named after famed mathematician George Boole). Both of the following expressions are valid:

```
_Bool flag = 0;
BOOL secondflag = 1;
```

4.7 **Objective-C Data Type Qualifiers**

So far we have looked at the basic data types offered within the context of the Objective-C programming language. We have seen that data types are provided for a number of different data declaration and storage needs and that each data type has associated with it some constraints in terms of what kind of data it can hold. In fact, it is possible to modify some of these constraints by using *qualifiers*. A number of such qualifiers are available and we will look at each one in turn in the remainder of this chapter.

4.7.1 long

The *long* qualifier is used to extend the value range of a data type. For example, to increase the range of an integer variable, the declaration is prefixed by the qualifier:

```
long int mylargeint;
```

The amount by which a data type's range is increased through the use of the long qualifier is system dependent, though on many modern systems *int* and *long int* both have the same range, making use of the qualifier unnecessary. The *long* qualifier may also be applied to the *double* data type. For example:

```
long double mydouble;
```

4.7.2 long long

It is safe to think of the *long long* qualifier as being equivalent to *extra long*. In the case of an *int* data type, the application of a *long long* qualifier typically will change the range from 32-bit up to 64-bit:

```
long long int mylargeint;
```

4.7.3 short

So far we have looked at qualifiers that increase the storage space, and thereby the value range, of data types. The *short* qualifier can be used to reduce the storage space and range of the *int* data type. This effectively reduces the integer to 16-bits in width, limiting the *signed* value range to −32,768 to +32,767:

```
short int myshort;
```

4.7.1 signed / unsigned

By default, an integer is assumed to be signed. In other words, the compiler assumes that an integer variable will be called upon to store either a negative or a positive number. This limits the extent that the range can reach in either direction. For example, a 32-bit *int* has a range of 4,294,967,295. In practice, because the value could be positive or negative the range is actually −2,147,483,648 to +2,147,483,647. If we know that a variable will never be called upon to store a negative value, we can declare it as unsigned, thereby extending the (positive) range to 0 to +4,294,967,295. An unsigned int is specified as follows:

```
unsigned int myint;
```

Qualifiers may also be combined, for example to declare an unsigned, short integer:

```
unsigned short int myint = 10;
```

Note that when using *unsigned*, *signed*, *short* and *long* with integer values, the *int* keyword is optional. The following are all valid:

```
short myint;
long myint;
unsigned myint;
signed myint;
```

4.8 **Summary**

Data types are the basic building blocks of just about every programming language and Objective-C is no exception. Now that we have covered these basics we will move on to the next chapter and begin talking about the use of variables.

Chapter 5

5. Working with Variables and Constants in Objective-C

In the previous chapter we looked at the basic data types supported by Objective-C. Perhaps the second most basic aspect of programming involves the use of variables and constants. Even the most advanced and impressive programs use variables in one form or another. In this chapter of *Objective-C 2.0 Essentials* we will cover everything that an Objective-C programmer needs to know about variables.

5.1 **What is an Objective-C Variable**

Variables are essentially locations in computer memory reserved for storing the data used by an application. Each variable is given a name by the programmer and assigned a value. The name assigned to the variable may then be used In the Objective-C code to access the value assigned to the variable. This access can involve either reading the value of the variable, or changing the value. It is, of course, the ability to change the value of variables which gives them the name *variable*.

A variable must be declared as a particular type such as an integer, a character, a float or double. Objective-C is what is known as a *strongly typed* language in that once a variable has been declared as a particular type it cannot subsequently be changed to a different type. While this may come as a shock to those familiar with loosely typed languages such as Ruby it will be familiar to Java, C, C++ or C# programmers. Whilst it is not possible to change the type of a variable it is possible to disguise the variable as another type under certain circumstances. This involves a concept known as *type casting* and will be covered later in this chapter.

Variable declarations require a type, a name and, optionally a value assignment. The following example declares an integer variable called *interestRate* but does not initialize it:

```
int interestRate;
```

The following example declares and initializes a variable using the assignment operator (=):

```
int interestRate = 10;
```

Similarly, a new value may be assigned to a variable at any point after it has been declared.

```
double interestRate = 5.5456; //Declare the variable and initialize
it to 5.5456
interestRate = 10.98; // variable now equals 10.98
interestRate = 20.87; // variable now equals 20.87
```

5.2 What is an Objective-C Constant?

A constant is similar to a variable in that it provides a named location in memory to store a data value. Constants differ in one significant way in that once a value has been assigned to a constant it cannot subsequently be changed.

Constants are particularly useful if there is a value which is used repeatedly throughout the application code. Rather than use the value each time, it makes the code easier to read if the value is first assigned to a constant which is then referenced in the code. For example, it might not be clear to someone reading your Objective-C code why you used the value 5 in an expression. If, instead of the value 5, you use a constant named *interestRate* the purpose of the value becomes much clearer. Constants also have the advantage that if the programmer needs to change a widely used value, it only needs to be changed once in the constant declaration and not each time it is referenced.

As with variables, constants have a type, a name and a value. Unlike variables, however, constants must be initialized at the same time that they are declared and must be prefixed with the const keyword:

```
const int interestRate = 10;
```

Once declared, it is not possible to assign a new value to the constant. The following code will cause the Objective-C compiler to report an error that reads "error: assignment of read-only variable":

```
const int interestRate = 10;
interestRate = 5; // invalid attempt to assign new value to read-only
const
```

Note that the value of a constant, unlike a variable, must be assigned at the point it is declared. For example, the following code will not compile:

```
const int interestRate;
interestRate = 10; // invalid attempt to initialize constant after
declaration
```

The above code will, once again, result in a compilation error.

5.3 Type Casting Objective-C Variables

As previously mentioned, Objective-C is a strongly typed language. In other words, once a variable has been declared as a specific data type, that type cannot be changed. It is possible, however, to make a variable behave as a different type using a concept known as *type casting*. Suppose we have two variables declared as doubles. We need to multiply these together and display the result:

```
double balance = 100.54;
double interestRate = 5.78;
double result = 0;


result = balance * interestRate;


NSLog (@"The result is %f", result);
```

When executed, we will get the following output:

```
The result is 581.121200
```

Now, suppose that we wanted the result to the nearest whole number. One option might, at first glance, appear to be to cast the two double values to integers within the arithmetic expression as follows:

```
double balance = 100.54;
double interestRate = 5.78;
double result;


result =  (int) balance *  (int) interestRate;
```

```
NSLog(@"The result is %f", result);
```

When compiled and run, however, the output will now read:

```
The result is 500.000000
```

Clearly this has not given us the result to the nearest whole number. This is because casting has not rounded the double values, but rather truncated the numbers at the decimal point resulting in the multiplication of 100 by 5. The correct code to perform the rounding is to use the *round()* function:

```
double balance = 100.54;
double interestRate = 5.78;

double result;

result = round(balance) * round(interestRate);

NSLog(@"The result is %f", result);
```

It is important to note that type casting only changes the way the value is read from the variable on that one occasion. It does not change the variable type or the value stored in any way. After the type cast, *balance* is still a *double* and still contains the value 100.54.

5.4 **Summary**

Variables and constants are essentially locations in computer memory reserved for the storage of data used by an application. Each variable and constant in an Objective-C program is given a name by the programmer and assigned a value. The name assigned may then be used in the Objective-C code to access the value assigned to the variable. Variables, as the name suggests, may be changed from within the code after being declared. The value assigned to a constant, on the other hand, cannot be changed after having been initialized to a particular value.

6. Objective-C Operators and Expressions

In the previous chapters we looked at using variables and constants in Objective-C and also described the different data types. Being able to create variables is only part of the story however. The next step is to learn how to use these variables and constants in Objective-C code. The primary method for working with data is in the form of *expressions*. In this chapter we will look in detail at Objective-C expressions and operators.

6.1 What is an Expression?

The most basic expression consists of an *operator*, two *operands* and an *assignment*. The following is an example of an expression:

```
int myresult = 1 + 2;
```

In the above example the (+) operator is used to add two operands (1 and 2) together. The *assignment operator* (=) subsequently assigns the result of the addition to an integer variable named *myresult*. The operands could just have easily been variables (or a mixture of constants and variables) instead of the actual numerical values used in the example.

In the remainder of this chapter we will look at the various types of operators available in Objective-C.

6.2 The Basic Assignment Operator

We have already looked at the most basic of assignment operators, the = operator. This assignment operator simply assigns the result of an expression to a variable. In essence, the = assignment operator takes two operands. The left hand operand is the variable to which a value is to be assigned and the right hand operand is the value to be assigned. The right hand operand is, more often than not, an expression which performs some type of arithmetic or logical evaluation, the result of which will be assigned to the variable. The following examples are all valid uses of the assignment operator:

```
int x; // declare the variable
x = 10;  // Assigns the value 10 to a variable named x
x = y + z; // Assigns the result of variable y added to variable z to
variable x
x = y;   // Assigns the value of variable y to variable x
```

Assignment operators may also be *chained* to assign the same value to multiple variables. For example, the following code example assigns the value 20 to the x, y and z variables:

```
int x, y, z;
x = y = z = 20;
```

6.3 **Objective-C Arithmetic Operators**

Objective-C provides a range of operators for the purpose of creating mathematical expressions. These operators primarily fall into the category of *binary* operators in that they take two operands. The exception is the *unary negative operator* (-) which serves to indicate that a value is negative rather than positive. This contrasts with the *subtraction operator* (-) which takes two operands (i.e. one value to be subtracted from another). For example:

```
int x = -10; // Unary - operator used to assign -10 to a variable
named x
x = y - z; // Subtraction operator. Subtracts z from y
```

The following table lists the primary Objective-C arithmetic operators:

Operator	Description
-(unary)	Negates the value of a variable or expression
*	Multiplication
/	Division
+	Addition
-	Subtraction
%	Modulo

Note that multiple operators may be used in a single expression.

For example:

```
x = y * 10 + z - 5 / 4;
```

Whilst the above code is perfectly valid, it is important to be aware that Objective-C does not evaluate the expression from left to right or right to left, but rather in an order specified by the precedence of the various operators. *Operator precedence* is an important topic to understand since it impacts the result of a calculation and will be covered in detail in *Objective-C 2.0 Operator Precedence.*

6.4 Compound Assignment Operators

In an earlier section we looked at the basic assignment operator (=). Objective-C provides a number of operators designed to combine an assignment with a mathematical or logical operation. These are primarily of use when performing an evaluation where the result is to be stored in one of the operands. For example, one might write an expression as follows:

```
x = x + y;
```

The above expression adds the value contained in variable x to the value contained in variable y and stores the result in variable x. This can be simplified using the addition compound assignment operator:

```
x += y
```

The above expression performs exactly the same task as *x = x + y* but saves the programmer some typing.

Numerous compound assignment operators are available in Objective-C. The most frequently used are outlined in the following table:

Operator	Description
x += y	Add x to y and place result in x
x -= y	Subtract y from x and place result in x
x *= y	Multiply x by y and place result in x
x /= y	Divide x by y and place result in x
x %= y	Perform Modulo on x and y and place result in x
x &= y	Assign to x the result of logical AND operation on x and y
x |= y	Assign to x the result of logical OR operation on x and y

| x ^= y | Assign to x the result of logical Exclusive OR on x and y |

6.5 **Increment and Decrement Operators**

Another useful shortcut can be achieved using the Objective-C increment and decrement operators (also referred to as *unary operators* because they operate on a single operand). As with the compound assignment operators described in the previous section, consider the following Objective-C code fragment:

```
x = x + 1; // Increase value of variable x by 1
x = x - 1; // Decrease value of variable x by 1
```

These expressions increment and decrement the value of x by 1. Instead of using this approach it is quicker to use the ++ and -- operators. The following examples perform exactly the same tasks as the examples above:

```
x++; Increment x by 1
x--; Decrement x by 1
```

These operators can be placed either before or after the variable name. If the operator is placed before the variable name, the increment or decrement is performed before any other operations are performed on the variable. For example, in the following example code, x is incremented before it is assigned to y, leaving y with a value of 10:

```
int x = 9;
int y;

y = ++x;
```

In the next example, however, the value of x (9) is assigned to variable y *before* the decrement is performed. After the expression is evaluated the value of y will be 9 and the value of x will be 8.

```
int x = 9;
int y;

y = x--;
```

6.6 **Comparison Operators**

In addition to mathematical and assignment operators, Objective-C also includes a set of logical operators useful for performing comparisons. These operators all return a Boolean (*BOOL*) *true* (1) or *false* (0) result depending on the result of the comparison. These operators are *binary operators* in that they work with two operands.

Comparison operators are most frequently used in constructing program flow control logic. For example an *if* statement may be constructed based on whether one value matches another:

```
if (x == y)
        // Perform task
```

The result of a comparison may also be stored in a *BOOL* variable. For example, the following code will result in a *true* (1) value being stored in the variable result:

```
BOOL result;
int x = 10;
int y = 20;

result = x < y;
```

Clearly 10 is less than 20, resulting in a *true* evaluation of the $x < y$ expression. The following table lists the full set of Objective-C comparison operators:

Operator	Description
x == y	Returns true if x is equal to y
x > y	Returns true if x is greater than y
x >= y	Returns true if x is greater than or equal to y
x < y	Returns true if x is less than y
x <= y	Returns true if x is less than or equal to y
x != y	Returns true if x is not equal to y

6.7 **Boolean Logical Operators**

Objective-C also provides a set of so called logical operators designed to return boolean *true* and *false*. In practice *true* equates to 1 and *false* equates to 0. These operators both return boolean results and take boolean values as operands. The key operators are NOT (!), AND (&&), OR (||) and XOR (^).

The NOT (!) operator simply inverts the current value of a boolean variable, or the result of an expression. For example, if a variable named *flag* is currently 1 (true), prefixing the variable with a '!' character will invert the value to 0 (false):

```
bool flag = true; //variable is true
bool secondFlag;


secondFlag = !flag; // secondFlag set to false
```

The OR (||) operator returns 1 if one of its two operands evaluates to *true*, otherwise it returns 0. For example, the following example evaluates to true because at least one of the expressions either side of the OR operator is true:

```
if ((10 < 20) || (20 < 10))
      NSLog (@"Expression is true");
```

The AND (&&) operator returns 1 only if both operands evaluate to be true. The following example code will return 0 because only one of the two operand expressions evaluates to *true*:

```
if ((10 < 20) && (20 < 10))
      NSLog (@"Expression is true");
```

The XOR (^) operator returns 1 if one and only one of the two operands evaluates to true. For example, the following example will return 1 since only one operator evaluates to be true:

```
if ((10 < 20) ^ (20 < 10))
      NSLog(@"Expression is true");
```

If both operands evaluated to be true or both were false the expression would return false.

6.8 **The Ternary Operator**

Objective-C uses something called a *ternary operator* to provide a shortcut way of making decisions. The syntax of the ternary operator (also known as the conditional operator) is as follows:

```
[condition] ? [true expression] : [false expression]
```

The way this works is that *[condition]* is replaced with an expression that will return either *true* (1) or *false* (0). If the result is true then the expression that replaces the *[true expression]* is evaluated. Conversely, if the result was *false* then the *[false expression]* is evaluated. Let's see this in action:

```
int x = 10;
int y = 20;


NSLog(@"Largest number is %i", x > y ? x : y );
```

The above code example will evaluate whether x is greater than y. Clearly this will evaluate to false resulting in y being returned to the NSLog call for display to the user:

```
2012-04-19 07:40:58.091 t[5724] Largest number is 20
```

6.9 **Bitwise Operators**

In *Objective-C 2.0 Data Types* we talked about the fact that computers work in binary. These are essentially streams of ones and zeros, each one referred to as a bit. Bits are formed into groups of 8 to form bytes. As such, it is not surprising that we, as programmers, will occasionally end up working at this level in our code. To facilitate this requirement, Objective-C provides a range of *bit operators*. Those familiar with bitwise operators in other languages such as C, C++, C# and Java will find nothing new in this area of the Objective-C language syntax. For those unfamiliar with binary numbers, now may be a good time to seek out reference materials on the subject in order to understand how ones and zeros are formed into bytes to form numbers. Other authors have done a much better job of describing the subject than we can do within the scope of this book.

For the purposes of this exercise we will be working with the binary representation of two numbers. Firstly, the decimal number 171 is represented in binary as:

```
10101011
```

Secondly, the number 3 is represented by the following binary sequence:

```
00000011
```

Now that we have two binary numbers with which to work, we can begin to look at the Objective-C's bitwise operators:

6.9.1 Bitwise AND

The Bitwise AND is represented by a single ampersand (&). It makes a bit by bit comparison of two numbers. Any corresponding position in the binary sequence of each number where both bits are 1 results in a 1 appearing in the same position of the resulting number. If either bit position contains a 0 then a zero appears in the result. Taking our two example numbers, this would appear as follows:

```
10101011 AND
00000011
========
00000011
```

As we can see, the only locations where both numbers have 1s are the last two positions. If we perform this in Objective-C code, therefore, we should find that the result is 3 (00000011):

```
int x = 171;
int y = 3;
int z;

z = x & y; // Perform a bitwise AND on the values held by variables x
and y

NSLog(@"Result is %i", z);

2009-10-07 15:38:09.176 t[12919] Result is 3
```

6.9.2 Bitwise OR

The bitwise OR also performs a bit by bit comparison of two binary sequences. Unlike the AND operation, the OR places a 1 in the result if there is a 1 in the first or second operand. The operator is represented by a single vertical bar character (|). Using our example numbers, the result will be as follows:

```
10101011 OR
00000011
========
10101011
```

If we perform this operation in an Objective-C example we see the following:

```
int x = 171;
int y = 3;
int z;

z = x | y;

NSLog(@"Result is %i", z);

2012-04-19 07:42:07.561 t[13153] Result is 171
```

6.9.3 Bitwise XOR

The bitwise XOR (commonly referred to as *exclusive OR* and represented by the caret '^' character) performs a similar task to the OR operation except that a 1 is placed in the result if one or other corresponding bit positions in the two numbers is 1. If both positions are a 1 or a 0 then the corresponding bit in the result is set to a 0. For example:

```
10101011 XOR
00000011
========
10101000
```

The result in this case is 10101000 which converts to 168 in decimal. To verify this we can, once again, try some Objective-C code:

```
int x = 171;
```

```
int y = 3;
int z;
z = x ^ y;
NSLog(@"Result is %i", z);
```

When executed, we get the following output from NSLog:

```
2012-04-19 07:42:39.562 t[13790] Result is 168
```

6.9.4 Bitwise Left Shift

The bitwise left shift moves each bit in a binary number a specified number of positions to the left. As the bits are shifted to the left, zeros are placed in the vacated right most (low order) positions. Note also that once the left most (high order) bits are shifted beyond the size of the variable containing the value, those high order bits are discarded:

```
10101011 Left Shift one bit
========
101010110
```

In Objective-C the bitwise left shift operator is represented by the '<<' sequence, followed by the number of bit positions to be shifted. For example, to shift left by 1 bit:

```
int x = 171;
int z;
z = x << 1;
NSLog(@"Result is %i", z);
```

When compiled and executed, the above code will display a message stating that the result is 342 which, when converted to binary, equates to 101010110.

6.9.5 Bitwise Right Shift

A bitwise right shift is, as you might expect, the same as a left except that the shift takes place in the opposite direction. Note that since we are shifting to the right there is no opportunity to retain the lower most bits regardless of the data type used to contain the result. As a result the low order bits are discarded. Whether or not the vacated high order bit positions are replaced with zeros or ones depends on whether the *sign bit* used to indicate positive and negative numbers is set or not and, unfortunately, on the particular system and Objective-C implementation in use.

```
10101011 Right Shift one bit
=========
01010101
```

The bitwise right shift is represented by the '>>' character sequence followed by the shift count:

```
int x = 171;
int z;
z = x >> 1;
NSLog(@"Result is %i", z);
```

When executed, the above code will report the result of the shift as being 85, which equates to binary 01010101.

6.10 Compound Bitwise Operators

As with the arithmetic operators, each bitwise operator has a corresponding compound operator that allows the operation and assignment to be performed using a single operator:

Operator	Description
x &= y	Perform a bitwise AND of x and y and assign result to x
x |= y	Perform a bitwise OR of x and y and assign result to x
x ^= y	Perform a bitwise XOR of x and y and assign result to x
x <<= n	Shift x left by n places and assign result to x
x >>= n	Shift x right by n places and assign result to x

6.11 Summary

Operators and expressions provide the underlying mechanism by which variables and constants are manipulated and evaluated within Objective-C code. This can take the simplest of forms whereby two numbers are added using the addition operator in an expression and the result stored in a variable using the assignment operator. Operators fall into a range of categories, details of which have been covered in some details in this chapter.

Chapter 7

7. Objective-C 2.0 Operator Precedence

In the previous chapter of *Objective-C 2.0 Essentials* we looked at Objective-C operators and expressions. An equally important area to understand is operator precedence. This is essentially the order in which Objective-C evaluates expressions comprising more than one operator.

7.1 An Example of Objective-C Operator Precedence

When humans evaluate expressions, they usually do so starting at the left of the expression and working towards the right. For example, working from left to right we get a result of 300 from the following expression:

```
10 + 20 * 10 - 300
```

This is because we, as humans, add 10 to 20, resulting in 30 and then multiply that by 10 to arrive at 300. Ask Objective-C to perform the same calculation and you get a very different answer:

```
int x = 10 + 20 * 10;
NSLog(@"Result is %i", x);
```

When executed, the result of the calculation is assigned to integer variable *x* and subsequently displayed using the NSLog call:

```
2012-04-19 07:43:50.165 t[3511] Result is 210
```

As we can see from the above output, Objective-C considers the answer to be 210. This is a direct result of *operator precedence*. Objective-C has a set of rules that tell it in which order operators should be evaluated in an expression. Clearly, Objective-C considers the multiplication operator (*) to be of a higher precedence than the addition (+) operator.

7.2 **Objective-C Operator Precedence and Associativity**

When addressing the issue of operator precedence in some scripting and programming languages, all that is generally required is a table listing the operators in order of precedence from highest to lowest. Objective-C has more in common with languages such as Java and C# in that operators are grouped together at different precedence levels. When operators from the same precedence level are found within the context of a single expression, a rule as to the order in which the operators are to be evaluated is followed. This rule is referred to as the *associativity* and differs from one group to the next. The following table outlines the operator precedence groups and corresponding associativity for Objective-C:

Operator	Description	Precedence	Associativity
[]	access array element or message expression	Highest	left to right
.	access object member or method		
()	invoke a method or function		
->	pointer to structure member		
++	increment		right to left
--	decrement		
+	unary plus		
-	unary minus		
!	logical NOT		
~	ones complement		
*	pointer reference		
&	address of		
sizeof	size of object		
(type)	type cast		
*	multiply		left to right
/	divide		
%	modulus		
+	add		left to right

–	subtract			
<< >> <	bitwise shift left bitwise shift right less than			left to right
<= >= >	less than or equal to greater than or equal to greater than			left to right
== !=	equality inequality			left to right
&	bitwise AND			left to right
^	bitwise XOR			left to right
|	bitwise OR			left to right
&&	logical AND			left to right
||	logical OR			left to right
?:	Conditional			right to left
= += – = *= /= %= &= ^= |= <<= >>= >>>=	assignment			right to left
,	comma		Lowest	right to left

As we can see from the table, when operators from the same precedence level appear in an expression, the operators are evaluated either left to right or right to left depending on the associativity of that group. For example, the following expression will be evaluated left to right because both operators are in the same precedence level and this is the rule dictated by the corresponding associativity:

```
int x = 10 * 20 / 5;
```

7.3 Overriding Operator Precedence

The precedence and associativity rules built into Objective-C can be overridden by surrounding the lower priority section of an expression with parentheses. For example, we can override precedence and force a left to right evaluation of our original example as follows:

```
int x = (10 + 20) * 10;
NSLog(@"Result is %i", x);
```

In the above example, the expression fragment enclosed in parentheses is evaluated before the higher precedence multiplication resulting in the expression equaling 300 instead of the 210 result we saw when we allowed precedence to take effect:

```
2012-04-19 07:44:23.642 t[5630] Result is 300
```

7.4 Summary

When humans evaluate expressions they typically do so from left to right. Such an assumption cannot, however, be made about the way in which expressions are evaluated by the Objective-C compiler. In actual fact, the order in which expressions are evaluated in Objective-C is dictated by strictly enforced sets of rules known as operator precedence and associativity. When required, the precedence of a section of an expression can be increased by encapsulating it in parentheses.

Chapter 8

8. Commenting Objective-C Code

There is an old saying amongst veteran programmers that goes something like "Don't comment bad code, re-write it!". Before exploring what these seasoned programmers are really saying, it is important to understand what comments are and why we should use them.

8.1 Why Comment your Code?

Comments in both programming and scripting languages provide a mechanism for the developer to write notes that are ignored by the compiler or interpreter. These notes are intended solely for either the developer or anyone else who may later need to modify the code. The main purpose of comments, therefore, is to allow the developer to make notes that help anyone who may read the code later to understand issues such as how a particular section of a program works, what a particular method does or what a variable is used to store. Commenting code is considered to be good practice. Rest assured that a section of Objective-C code that seems obvious when you write it will often be confusing when you return to it months, or even years later to modify it. By including explanatory comments alongside the code this becomes less of a problem.

Now, back to that old saying - "Don't comment bad code, re-write it!". What this phrase suggests is that if code is well written in the first place you do not need comments to explain what it does and how it does it. It also suggests that if you have to write lots of comments to explain what a section of your Objective-C program does then you must have written it badly. Whilst one should always strive to write good code there is absolutely nothing wrong with including comments to explain what the code does. Even a well written program can be difficult to understand if it is solving a difficult problem, so ignore the old programmer's adage and never hesitate to comment your Objective-C code.

Another useful application of comments in Objective-C is to *comment out* sections of a program. Putting comment markers around sections of code ensures that they are ignored by the compiler during compilation. This can be especially useful when you are debugging a program and want to try out something different, but do not want to have to delete the old code until you have tested that the new code actually works.

8.2 **Single Line Comments**

The mechanism for a single line comment is marked by prefixing the line with // (this will be familiar to C++ or Java programmers). For example:

```
// This is a comment line. It is for human use only and is ignored by
the Objective-C compiler.
NSString *myString;
int i = 0;
// This is another comment
```

The // syntax tells the compiler that everything on the same line following on from the // is a comment and should be ignored. This means that anything on the line before the // comment marker is *not* ignored. The advantage of this is that it enables comments to be placed at the end of a line of code. For example:

```
NSString *myString = @"Welcome to Techotopia"; // Variable containing
pointer to welcome string object
```

In the above example everything after the // marker is considered a comment and, therefore, ignored by the Objective-C compiler. This provides an ideal method for placing comments on the same line of code that describe what that particular line of code does.

8.3 **Multi-line Comments**

For the purposes of supporting comments that extend over multiple lines Objective-C borrowed some syntax from the C programming language. The start and end of lines of comments are marked by the /* and */ markers respectively. Everything immediately after the /* and before the */ is considered to be a comment, regardless of where the markers appear on a line. For example:

```
/*
This Function adds two numbers together
and returns the result of the addition
```

```
*/

(int) addNums (num1, num2)
{
        return (num1 + num2)
}
```

Multi-line comments are particularly useful for commenting out sections of a program you no longer wish to run but do not yet wish to delete, together with an explanation of when and why you have commented it out:

```
/*
Commented out December 23 while testing improved version
int myValue = 1;
NSString *myString = @"My lucky number is ";
NSLog ( @"%@ %@", myString, myValue );
*/
```

In the above example everything between the /* and */ markers is considered to be a comment. Even though this content contains valid Objective-C code it is ignored by the compiler.

8.4 Summary

Comments in Objective-C enable the developer to add notes about the code or *comment out* sections of code that should not be compiled. Comments can be single line comments (using the // marker) or multi-line (beginning with /* and ending with */).

Commenting is considered to be good practice. Regardless of how well you understand the logic of some Objective-C, there is a good chance you may one day have to return to that code and modify it. Often this can be months, or even years later and what seemed obvious to you at the time you wrote it may seem less obvious in the future. Also, it is often likely that some other person will have to work on your code in the future. For both these reasons it is a good idea to provide at least some basic amount of commenting in your code.

9. Objective-C Flow Control with *if* and *else*

In the *Objective-C Operators and Expressions* chapter, we looked at how to use logical expressions in Objective-C to determine whether something is *true* or *false*. Since programming is largely an exercise in applying logic, much of the art of programming involves writing code that makes decisions based on one or more criteria. Such decisions define which code gets executed and, conversely, which code gets by-passed when the program is executing. This is often referred to as *flow control* since it controls the *flow* of program execution.

In previous chapters the *if* statement has been used in some examples. In this chapter of *Objective-C 2.0 Essentials* we are going to look at *if* statements in a little more detail.

9.1 Using the if Statement

The *if* statement is perhaps the most basic of flow control options available to the Objective-C programmer. Programmers who are familiar with C, C++ or Java will immediately be comfortable using Objective-C *if* statements.

The basic syntax of the Objective-C *if* statement is as follows:

```
if (boolean expression) {
// Objective-C code to be performed when expression evaluates to true
}
```

Note that the braces ({}) are only required if more than one line of code is executed after the *if* expression. If only one line of code is listed under the *if* the braces are optional. For example, the following code is valid:

```
int x = 10;

if (x > 10)
```

```
        x = 10;
```

Essentially if the *boolean expression* evaluates to 1 (*true*) then the code in the body of the statement is executed (see *Objective-C Operators and Expressions* for more details of this type of logic). The body of the statement is enclosed in braces ({}). If, on the other hand, the expression evaluates to 0 (*false*) the code in the body of the statement is skipped.

For example, if a decision needs to be made depending on whether one value is greater than another, we would write code similar to the following:

```
int x = 10;

if ( x > 9 )
{
        NSLog (@"x is greater than 9!");
}
```

Clearly, x is indeed greater than 9 causing the message to appear in the console window.

9.2 Using if ... else ... Statements

The next variation of the *if* statement allows us to also specify some code to perform if the expression in the *if* statement evaluates to *false*. The syntax for this construct is as follows:

```
if (boolean expression) {
// Code to be executed if expression is true
} else {
// Code to be executed if expression is false
}
```

Using the above syntax, we can now extend our previous example to display a different message if the comparison expression evaluates to be *false*:

```
int x = 10;

if ( x > 9 )
{
        NSLog (@"x is greater than 9!");
```

```
} else {
        NSLog (@"x is less than 9!");

}
```

In this case, the second NSLog statement would execute if the value of x was less than 9.

9.3 **Using if ... else if ... Statements**

So far we have looked at *if* statements which make decisions based on the result of a single logical expression. Sometimes it becomes necessary to make decisions based on a number of different criteria. For this purpose we can use the *if ... else if ...* construct, the syntax for which is as follows:

```
int x = 9;

if (x == 10)
{
        NSLog (@"x is 10");
}
else if (x == 9)
{
NSLog (@"x is 9");
}
else if (x == 8)
{
        NSLog (@"x is 8");
}
```

This approach works well for a moderate number of comparisons, but can become cumbersome for a larger volume of expression evaluations. For such situations, the Objective-C *switch* statement provides a more flexible and efficient solution. For more details on using the *switch* statement read the chapter entitled *The Objective-C switch Statement*.

9.4 **Summary**

In this chapter we looked at the use of Objective-C *if* statements including if, if ... else and if ... else if ... constructs. In the next chapter of this book we will look at using the Objective-C *switch* statement as an alternative to more complex if statements.

Chapter 10

10. The Objective-C *switch* Statement

In *Objective-C Flow Control with if and else* we looked at how to control program execution flow using the *if* and *else* statements. Whilst these statement constructs work well for testing a limited number of conditions, they quickly become unwieldy when dealing with larger numbers of possible conditions. To simplify such situations, Objective-C has inherited the *switch* statement from the C programming language. In this chapter we will explore the *switch* statement in detail.

10.1 Why Use a switch Statement?

For a small number of logical evaluations of a value the *if ... else if ...* construct outlined in *Objective-C Flow Control with if and else* is perfectly adequate. Unfortunately, any more than two or three possible scenarios can quickly make such a construct both time consuming to write and difficult to read. As a case in point consider the following code example. The program is designed to evaluate integers between 0 and 5 entered at the keyboard and to output the word version of the number (zero, one, two etc):

```
int value;

printf ("Enter a number between 0 and 5: ");
scanf ("%i", &value);

if (value == 0)
    NSLog (@"zero");
else if (value == 1)
    NSLog (@"one");
else if (value == 2)
    NSLog (@"two");
else if (value == 3)
    NSLog (@"three");
```

```
      else if (value == 4)
        NSLog (@"four");
      else if (value == 5)
        NSLog (@"five");
      else
        NSLog (@"Integer out of range");
```

As you can see, whilst the code is not too excessive it is already starting to become somewhat hard to read and also took more time to write than should really be necessary. Imagine, however, if instead of five numbers we had to test for more. Clearly an easier solution is needed, and that solution is the *switch* statement.

10.2 **Using the switch Statement Syntax**

The syntax for an Objective-C *switch* statement is as follows:

```
switch (expression)
{
    case match1:
        statements
        break;

    case match2:
        statements
        break;
    default:
        statements
        break;
}
```

This syntax needs a little explanation before we embark on creating a *switch* based version of the above *if ... else* construct.

In the above syntax outline, *expression* represents either a value, or an expression which returns a value. This is the value against which the *switch* operates. Using our example, this would be the integer to be evaluated.

For each possible match a *case* statement is required, followed by a *match* value. Each potential match must be of the same type as the governing expression. Following on from the *case* line are the Objective-C statements that are to be executed in the event of the value matching the case match.

After the *statements* comes a *break* statement. This statement breaks out of the switch statement. Failure to provide a break statement results in every case after the matching case evaluating to true (regardless of whether the match is made or not) and the corresponding Objective-C statements executing.

Finally, the *default* section of the construct defines what should happen if none of the case statements present a match to the *expression*.

10.3 A switch Statement Example

With the above information in mind we may now construct a *switch* statement that provides the same functionality as our previous and somewhat unwieldy *if ... else if ...* construct:

```
int value;


printf ("Enter a number between 0 and 5: ");
scanf ("%i", &value);


switch (value)
{
    case 0:
        NSLog (@"zero");
        break;
    case 1:
        NSLog (@"one");
        break;
    case 2:
        NSLog (@"two");
        break;
    case 3:
        NSLog (@"three");
```

```
        break;
    case 4:
        NSLog (@"four");
        break;
    case 5:
        NSLog (@"five");
   break;
    default:
        NSLog (@"Integer out of range");
        break;
}
```

10.4 **Explaining the Example**

When compiled and run, the sample application will prompt for a number between 0 and 5. Once entered, the response is assigned to the integer variable *value* which in turn is used as the *governing variable* in the *switch* statement.

The *default* option simply displays an out of range message if none of the case statements match the number entered by the user.

10.5 **Combining case Statements**

In the above example, each case had its own set of statements to execute. Sometimes a number of different matches may require the same code to be executed. In this case, it is possible to group case statements together with a common set of statements to be executed when a match for any of the cases is found. For example, we can modify the switch construct in our example so that the same code is executed regardless of whether the user enters 0, 1 or 2:

```
switch (value)
{
    case 0:
    case 1:
    case 2:
      NSLog (@"zero, one or two");
      break;
```

```
    case 3:
      NSLog (@"three");
      break;
    case 4:
      NSLog (@"four");
      break;
    case 5:
      NSLog (@"five");
  break;
    default:
      NSLog (@"Integer out of range");
      break;
  }
```

10.6 **Summary**

Whilst the *if.. else..* construct serves as a good decision making option for small numbers of possible outcomes, this approach can become unwieldy in more complex situations. An alternative method for implementing flow control logic in Objective-C when many possible outcomes exist as the result of an evaluation, the switch statement often makes a more suitable option.

11. Objective-C Looping - The *for* Statement

In this chapter of *Objective-C 2.0 Essentials* we will continue looking at flow control in Objective-C applications. In the preceding chapters we have looked in detail at using logical expressions to decide what code should be executed. Another aspect of flow control entails the definition of loops. Loops are essentially sequences of Objective-C statements which are to be executed repeatedly until a specified condition is met.

11.1 Why Use Loops?

It is generally common knowledge that computers are great at performing repetitive tasks an infinite number of times, and doing so very quickly. It is also common knowledge that computers really don't do anything unless someone programs them to tell them what to do. Loop statements are the primary mechanism for telling a computer that a sequence of tasks needs to be repeated a specific number of times. Suppose, for example, that you have a requirement to add a number to itself ten times. One way to do this might be to write the following Objective-C code:

```
int j = 10;

j += j;
j += j;
j += j;
j += j;
j += j;
j += j;
j += j;
j += j;
j += j;
j += j;
```

Objective-C Looping - The for Statement

Whilst this is somewhat cumbersome, it does work. What would happen, however, if you needed to perform this task 100 or even 10,000 times? Writing Objective-C code to perform this as above would be prohibitive. Such a scenario is exactly what the *for* loop is intended to handle.

The syntax of an Objective-C *for loop* is as follows:

```
for ( ''initializer''; ''conditional expression''; ''loop
expression'' )
{
     // statements to be executed
}
```

The *initializer* typically initializes a counter variable. Traditionally the variable name *i* is used for this purpose, though any valid variable name will do. For example:

```
i = 0;
```

This sets the counter to be the variable *i* and sets it to zero. Note that the previously widely used Objective-C standard (c89) required that this variable be declared prior to its use in the *for* loop. For example:

```
int i=0;

for (i = 0; i < 10; i++)
{
     // Statements here
}
```

The current standard (c99) allows the variable to be declared and initialized in the *for* loop as follows:

```
for (int i=0; i<10; i++)
{
    //Statements here
}
```

If you compile code containing this construct using a c89 level compiler you may get an error similar to the following:

```
error: 'for' loop initial declaration used outside C99 mode
```

If you do see this message, you should be able to switch into C99 mode by adding the -*std=c99* command-line flag to your compilation command. For example:

```
clang -std=c99 -framework Foundation hello.m -o hello
```

The *conditional expression* specifies the test to perform to verify whether the loop has been performed the required number of iterations. For example, if we want to loop 10 times:

```
i < 10;
```

Finally the *loop expression* specifies the action to perform on the counter variable. For example to increment by 1:

```
i++;
```

The body of statements to be executed on each iteration of the loop is contained within the code block defined by the opening ({) and closing (}) braces. If only one statement is to be executed the braces are optional, though still recommended for code readability and so that you don't forget to add them if you later increase the number of statements to be performed in the loop.

Bringing this all together we can create a *for* loop to perform the task outlined in the earlier example:

```
int j = 10;

for (int i=0; i<10; i++)
{
    j += j;
}

NSLog (@"j = %i", j);
```

11.2 **Objective-C Loop Variable Scope**

A key point to note in creating loops is that any variables defined within the body of a loop are only visible to code within the loop. This is a concept known as *scope*. If, for example, a variable *myCounter* is defined in a *for* loop, that variable ceases to exist once the loop terminates:

```
// variable myCounter does not yet exist

for (int i = 0; i < 10; i++)
{
        int myCounter = 0; //myCounter variable created in scope of
for loop
        myCounter += i;
}
// after loop exit variable myCounter is now out of scope and ceases
to exist
```

11.3 **Creating an Infinite *for* Loop**

A *for* loop that will execute an infinite number of times may be constructed using *for (;;)* syntax. For example, the following code sample will output *Hello from Objective-C* until the program is manually terminated by the user (or the computer is turned off or rebooted):

```
for (;;)
{
    NSLog (@"Hello from Objective-C");
}
```

11.4 **Breaking Out of a *for* Loop**

Having created a loop, it is possible that under certain conditions you might want to break out of the loop before the completion criteria have been met (particularly if you have created an infinite loop). One such example might involve continually checking for activity on a network socket. Once activity has been detected it will be necessary to break out of the monitoring loop and perform some other task.

For the purpose of breaking out of a loop, Objective-C provides the *break* statement which breaks out of the current loop and resumes execution at the code directly after the loop. For example:

```
int j = 10;

for (int i = 0; i < 100; i++)
{
    j += j;

    if (j > 100)
        break;

    NSLog (@"j = %i", j);
}
```

In the above example the loop will continue to execute until the value of j exceeds 100 at which point the loop will exit.

11.5 Nested *for* Loops

So far we have looked at only a single level of *for* loop. It is also possible to nest *for* loops where one *for* loop resides inside another *for* loop. Consider, for example, the following code excerpt:

```
int j;

for (int i = 0; i < 100; i++)
{
    NSLog ( @"i = %i", i);

    for (j = 0; j < 10; j++)
    {
        NSLog ( @"j = %i", j);
    }
}
```

The above example will loop 100 times displaying the value of *i* on each iteration. In addition, for each of those iterations it will loop 10 times displaying the value of *j*.

11.6 **Breaking from Nested Loops**

An important point to be aware of when breaking out of a nested *for* loop is that the break only exits from the current level of loop. For example, the following Objective-C code example will exit from the current iteration of the nested loop when *j* is equal to 5. The outer loop will, however, continue to iterate and, in turn execute the nested loop:

```objc
for (int i = 0; i < 100; i++)
{
    NSLog( @"i = %i", i);

    for (int j = 0; j < 10; j++)
    {
        if (j == 5)
            break;

        NSLog ( @"j = %i", j);
    }
}
```

11.7 **Continuing** *for* **Loops**

Another useful statement for use in loops is the *continue* statement. When the execution process finds a *continue* statement in any kind of loop, it skips all remaining code in the body of the loop and begins execution once again from the top of the loop. Using this technique we can, for example, construct a *for* loop which outputs only even numbers between 1 and 9:

```objc
for (int i = 1; i < 10; i++)
{
    if ((i % 2) != 0)
        continue;

    NSLog( @"i = %i", i);
```

```
}
```

In the example, if *i* is not divisible by 2 with 0 remaining the code performs a *continue* operation sending execution to the top of the *for* loop, thereby bypassing the code to output the value of *i*. This will result in the following output:

```
2
4
6
8
```

11.8 Using *for* Loops with Multiple Variables

In the examples we have covered so far we have used a single variable within the *for* loop construct. Objective-C actually permits multiple variables to be modified within the looping process. In the following example, the *for* loop increments two variables, *i* and *j*:

```
int j;
int i;

for (j = 0, i = 0; i < 10; i++, j++)
{
        NSLog( @"i = %i, j = %i", i, j);
}
```

Note that although both *i* and *j* are initialized and incremented in this loop, the number of times the loop is to be performed is still based on the value of *i* through the *i* < *10* expression. The initialization and modification expressions for additional variables do not need to be the same as the control variable. For example, the following example initializes *j* to 5 and multiplies it by 2:

```
int j;
int i;

for (j = 5, i = 0; i < 10; i++, j *= 2)
{
        NSLog( @"i = %i, j = %i", i, j);
```

```
}
```

When the above loop is executed we get output similar to:

```
2012-11-19 14:55:15.892 main[39080:707] i = 0, j = 5
2012-11-19 14:55:15.894 main[39080:707] i = 1, j = 10
2012-11-19 14:55:15.895 main[39080:707] i = 2, j = 20
2012-11-19 14:55:15.895 main[39080:707] i = 3, j = 40
2012-11-19 14:55:15.896 main[39080:707] i = 4, j = 80
2012-11-19 14:55:15.897 main[39080:707] i = 5, j = 160
2012-11-19 14:55:15.897 main[39080:707] i = 6, j = 320
2012-11-19 14:55:15.898 main[39080:707] i = 7, j = 640
2012-11-19 14:55:15.898 main[39080:707] i = 8, j = 1280
2012-11-19 14:55:15.899 main[39080:707] i = 9, j = 2560
```

11.9 **Summary**

Computers excel at performing repetitive tasks multiple times. One of the most common mechanisms for implementing looping in an Objective-C application is to make use of the *for* statement. The *for* statement construct is ideal for executing a particular block of code a specific number of times. This chapter has covered the basics of *for* loops in addition to more advanced topics such as nested *for* loops, loops with multiple variables, variable scope and the roles of the *break* and *continue* statements.

12. Objective-C Looping with *do* and *while* Statements

The Objective-C *for* loop described previously works well when you know in advance how many times a particular task needs to be repeated in a program. There will, however, be instances where code needs to be repeated until a certain condition is met, with no way of knowing in advance how many repetitions are going to be needed to meet that criteria. To address this need, Objective-C provides the *while* loop (yet another construct inherited by Objective-C from the C Programming Language).

12.1 The Objective-C while Loop

Essentially, the *while* loop repeats a set of tasks until a specified condition is met. The *while* loop syntax is defined as follows:

```
while (''condition'')
{
    // Objective-C statements go here
}
```

In the above syntax, *condition* is an expression that will return either *true* (1) or *false* (0) and the *// Objective-C statements go here* comment represents the code to be executed while the *condition* expression is *true*. For example:

```
int myCount = 0;

while ( myCount < 100 )
{
    myCount++;
}
```

In the above example, the *while* expression will evaluate whether the *myCount* variable is less than 100. If it is already greater than 100 the code in the braces is skipped and the loop exits without performing any tasks.

If, on the other hand, *myCount* is not greater than 100 the code in the braces is executed and the loop returns to the *while* statement and repeats the evaluation of *myCount*. This process repeats until the value of *myCount* is greater than 100, at which point the loop exits.

12.2 **Objective-C *do ... while* loops**

It is often helpful to think of the *do ... while* loop as an inverted *while* loop. The *while* loop evaluates an expression before executing the code contained in the body of the loop. If the expression evaluates to *false* on the first check then the code is not executed. The *do ... while* loop, on the other hand, is provided for situations where you know that the code contained in the body of the loop will *always* need to be executed at least once. For example, you may want to keep stepping through the items in an array until a specific item is found. You know that you have to at least check the first item in the array to have any hope of finding the entry you need. The syntax for the *do ... while* loop is as follows:

```
do
{
        // Objective-C statements here
} while (''conditional expression'');
```

In the *do ... while* example below the loop will continue until the value of a variable named *i* equals 0:

```
int i = 10;
do
{
        i--;
} while (i > 0);
```

12.3 **Breaking from Loops**

As with the *for* loop, it is also possible to exit from a *while* or *do while* loop at any time through the use of the *break* statement. When the execution path encounters a *break* statement, the looping will stop and execution will proceed to the code immediately following the loop. In the following example, the loop is coded to exit when the value of *i* matches the value of *j*:

```
int i = 0;
int j = 5;

while (i < 100)
{
    i++;

    if (i == j)
        break;
}
```

It is important to note that in the case of nested loops the *break* statement only exits the current loop leaving the outer loop to continue executing (and most likely once again executing the inner loop).

12.4 The *continue* Statement

The *continue* statement causes all remaining code statements in a loop to be skipped, and execution to be returned to the top of the loop. In the following example, the NSLog function is only called when the value of variable *i* is an even number (i.e. divisible by 2 with no remainder):

```
int i = 1;

while (i < 20)
{
    i++;
    if ((i % 2) != 0)
        continue;
    NSLog (@"i = %i", i);
}
```

The *continue* statement in the above example will cause the NSLog call to be skipped unless the value of *i* can be divided by 2 with no remainder. If the *continue* statement is triggered, execution will skip to the top of the while loop and the statements in the body of the loop will be repeated (until the value of *i* exceeds 19), resulting in the following output:

```
i = 2
i = 4
i = 6
i = 8
i = 10
i = 12
i = 14
i = 16
i = 18
i = 20
```

12.5 Summary

The Objective-C *while* and *do…while* looping constructs provide an alternative to the *for* loop in situations where it is not possible to know in advance how many times the loop will need to be performed to meet a specified criteria. The condition under which the loop exits is controlled by the Boolean result of a test or expression evaluating to true. As with the *for* loop, both the *break* and *continue* statements can be used from within the loop to control the execution flow.

13. An Overview of Objective-C Object Oriented Programming

So far we have looked at the basics of programming in Objective-C such as variable types, flow control and looping. Although it would be possible to write a functional program using these techniques, there is much more to becoming a proficient Objective-C programmer. Objective-C is, above all, an object oriented programming language and as such any Objective-C programmer will be expected to create object-oriented applications using this language.

Aside from needing to learn about object oriented programming in order to create your own objects, you will also find that working with entities such as strings, arrays and files in Objective-C will also require an understanding of how to work with objects.

Objective-C provides extensive support for developing object-oriented applications. The subject area of object oriented programming is, however, large. It is not an exaggeration to state that entire books have been dedicated to the subject. As such, a detailed overview of object oriented software development is beyond the scope of this book. Instead, we will introduce the basic concepts involved in object oriented programming and then move on to explaining the concept as it relates to Objective-C application development.

13.1 What is an Object?

Objects are self-contained pieces of functionality that can be easily used, and re-used as the building blocks for a software application.

Objects consist of data variables and functions (called *methods*) that can be accessed and called on the object to perform tasks. These are collectively referred to as *members*.

13.2 **What is a Class?**

Much as a blueprint or architect's drawing defines what an item or a building will look like once it has been constructed, a class defines what an object will look like when it is created. It defines, for example, what the *methods* will do and what the *member* variables will be.

13.3 **Creating the Example Project**

For the purposes of this chapter a new Xcode project will be required. Begin, therefore, by launching Xcode and selecting the option to *Create a New Project.* In the new project panel, select the *Application* option listed beneath OS X in the left hand pane, followed by *Command Line Tool* in the main pane before clicking on *Next.* Enter *BankAccount* as the product name, verify that the *Type* menu is set to *Foundation* and that *Automatic Reference Counting* is enabled. Click the *Next* button, choose a suitable file system location for the project files and then click *Create.*

In the event that you are learning Objective-C on a platform which does not support Xcode, simply use your preferred editor to create the files outlined in this chapter.

13.4 **Declaring an Objective-C Class Interface**

Before an object can be instantiated, we first need to define the class 'blueprint' for the object. In this chapter we will create a Bank Account class to demonstrate the basic concepts of Objective-C object oriented programming.

An Objective-C class is defined in terms of an *interface* and an *implementation*. In the interface section of the definition we specify the base class from which the new class is to be derived and also define the members and methods that the class will contain. The syntax for the interface section of a class is as follows:

```
@interface NewClassName: ParentClass {
   // Instance Variables
}
// Method Declarations
@end
```

The *Instance Variables* section of the interface defines the variables that are to be contained within the class. These variables are declared in the same way that any other variable would be declared in Objective-C.

The *Method Declarations* section, on the other hand, defines the methods that are available to be called on the class. These are essentially functions specific to the class that perform a particular operation when called upon.

To create an example outline interface section for our BankAccount class, we would use the following:

```
@interface BankAccount: NSObject
{

}
@end
```

The parent class chosen above is the *NSObject* class. This is a standard base class provided with the Objective-C Foundation framework and is the class from which most new classes are derived. By deriving BankAccount from this parent class, we inherit a range of additional methods used in creating, managing and destroying instances that we would otherwise have to write ourselves.

The next step is to add the new class to our Xcode project. This can be achieved by Ctrl-clicking on the *BankAccount* entry located at the top of the Project Navigator panel and selecting *New File...* from the menu. Alternatively, select *File -> New -> File...* from the Xcode menu bar at the top of the screen. Once invoked, the new file panel illustrated in Figure 13-1 will appear:

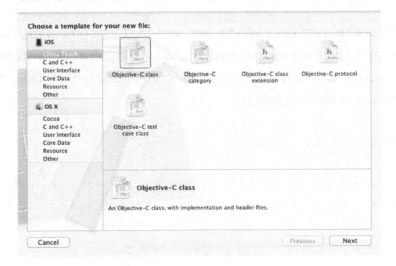

Figure 13-1

Since we are adding a new class to the project, select the *Objective-C class* entry before clicking *Next*. On the subsequent panel, enter *BankAccount* into the Class field and change the *Subclass of* menu to *NSObject*. Click *Next,* select a location for the new class files and click on *Create*.

A review of the files in the Project Navigator panel will reveal that Xcode has added both interface (*BankAccount.h*) and implementation (*BankAccount.m*) files to the project. Select the *BankAccount.h* file and note that it contains the outline of the new class:

```
#import <Foundation/Foundation.h>


@interface BankAccount : NSObject


@end
```

Now that we have the outline syntax for our class, the next step is to add some instance variables to it.

13.5 **Adding Instance Variables to a Class**

A key objective of object oriented programming is a concept referred to as *data encapsulation*. The idea behind data encapsulation is that data should be stored within classes and accessed only through methods defined in that class. Data encapsulated in a class are referred to as *instance variables* (commonly abbreviated to *ivars*).

Instances of our BankAccount class will be required to store some data, specifically a bank account number and the balance currently held by the account. Instance variables are declared in the same way any other variables are declared in Objective-C. We can, therefore, add these variables as follows:

```
@interface BankAccount: NSObject
{
        double accountBalance;
        long accountNumber;
}
@end
```

Having defined our instance variables, we can now move on to defining the methods of the class that will allow us to work with our instance variables while staying true to the data encapsulation model.

13.6 **Defining Instance Methods**

The methods of a class are essentially code routines that can be called upon to perform specific tasks within the context of an instance of that class.

Methods come in two different forms, *class methods* and *instance methods*. Class methods operate at the level of the class, such as creating a new instance of a class and are covered in more detail in *Writing Objective-C Class Methods*. Instance methods, on the other hand, operate only on the instance of a class (for example performing an arithmetic operation on two instance variables and returning the result). *Class methods* are preceded by a plus (+) sign in the declaration and instance methods are preceded by a minus (-) sign. If the method returns a result, the name of the method must be preceded by the data type returned enclosed in parentheses. If a method does not return a result, then the method must be declared as *void*. If data needs to be passed through to the method (referred to as *arguments*), the method name is followed by a colon, the data type in parentheses and a name for the argument. For example, the declaration of a method to set the account number in our example might read as follows:

```
-(void) setAccountNumber: (long) y;
```

The method is an *instance method* so it is preceded by the minus sign. It does not return a result so it is declared as *(void)*. It takes an argument (the account number) of type *long* so we follow the *accountNumber* name with a colon (:) specify the argument type *(long)* and give the argument a name (in this case we simply use *y*).

The following method is intended to return the current value of the account number instance variable (which is of type *long*):

```
-(long) getAccountNumber;
```

Methods may also be defined to accept more than one argument. For example to define a method that accepts both the account number and account balance we could declare it as follows:

```
-(void) setAccount: (long) y andBalance: (double) x;
```

Now that we have an understanding of the structure of method declarations within the context of the class *interface* definition, we can extend our BankAccount class accordingly. Within Xcode, select the *BankAccount.h* interface file and modify it to add method declarations:

```
@interface BankAccount: NSObject
{
        double accountBalance;
        long accountNumber;
}
-(void) setAccount: (long) y andBalance: (double) x;
-(void) setAccountBalance: (double) x;
-(double) getAccountBalance;
-(void) setAccountNumber: (long) y;
-(long) getAccountNumber;
-(void) displayAccountInfo;
@end
```

Having defined the interface, we are almost ready to move on to defining the *implementation* of our class. First, however, it is necessary to explain the concept of controlling access to instance variables

13.7 **Controlling Access to Instance Variables**

By default, instance variables in a class can only be accessed by the methods of that class. This is the default for instance variables and is called *protected access*. A number of access options are available:

- **protected** - Access is allowed only by methods of the class and any subclasses.
- **private** - Access is restricted to methods of the class. Access is not available to subclasses.
- **public** - Direct access is available to methods of the class, subclasses and code in other module files and classes.

The access level for instance variables is specified in the @interface section of the class declaration using the *@protected*, *@private* and *@public* directives. Once a directive has been specified, all instance variables beneath that line adopt that setting until another directive is specified. For example:

```
@interface
{
     double accountBalance;
@private
     long accountNumber;
     int accessCount;
@public
     float interestRate;
}
```

In the above example, *accountBalance* will default to *protected access* since it is not preceded by a directive, *accountNumber* and *accessCount* are both *private* and *interestRate* is *public*.

When accessing a public instance variable from another class or any other code in a method or function, the -> pointer operator notation is used.

For example:

```
account1->interestRate = 0.67;
```

Keep in mind that an attempt to access a non-public instance variable using pointer notation will result in a compiler warning. For example, consider the following code fragment:

```
account1->accountBalance = 12345.67;
```

When compiled, the above line of code will generate a warning from the compiler since *accountBalance* is protected and should not, therefore, be accessed in this way.

```
warning: instance variable 'accountNumber' is @protected; this will be a
hard error in the future
```

Whilst the code will compile and run with the current version of the compiler, as the message suggests this will be considered a hard syntax error in future releases of the Objective-C compiler thereby causing compilation to fail.

13.8 **Declaring an Objective-C Class Implementation**

The next step in creating a new class in Objective-C is to write the code for the methods we have already declared. This is performed in the *@implementation* section of the class definition. An outline implementation is structured as follows:

```
@implementation NewClassName
    // Methods
@end
```

In order to implement the methods we declared in the *@interface* section, therefore, we need to modify the BankAccount.m implementation file as follows:

```
#import "BankAccount.h"

@implementation BankAccount

-(void) setAccount: (long) y andBalance: (double) x;
{
        accountBalance = x;
        accountNumber = y;
}
-(void) setAccountBalance: (double) x
{
        accountBalance = x;
}

-(double) getAccountBalance
{

        return accountBalance;
}


-(void) setAccountNumber: (long) y
```

```
{
     accountNumber = y;
}


-(long) getAccountNumber
{
     return accountNumber;
}


-(void) displayAccountInfo
{
     NSLog (@"Account Number %ld has a balance of %f",
accountNumber, accountBalance);
}
@end
```

We are now at the point where we can write some code to work with our new BankAccount class.

13.9 Declaring, Initializing and Releasing a Class Instance

So far all we have done is define the blueprint for our class. In order to do anything with this class, we need to create instances of it. The first step in this process is to declare a variable to store a pointer to the instance when it is created. We do this as follows:

```
BankAccount *account1;
```

Having created a variable to store a reference to the class instance, we can now allocate memory in preparation for initializing the class:

```
account1 = [BankAccount alloc];
```

In the above statement we are calling the *alloc* method of the BankAccount class (note that *alloc* is a *class method* inherited from the parent *NSObject* class, as opposed to an *instance method* created by us in the BankAccount class).

Having allocated memory for the class instance, the next step is to initialize the instance by calling the *init* class method:

```
account1 = [account1 init];
```

For the sake of economy of typing, the above three statements are frequently rolled into a single line of code as follows:

```
BankAccount *account1 = [[BankAccount alloc] init];
```

In the first step of this section we allocated memory for the creation of the class instance. Good programming conventions dictate that memory allocated to a class instance should be released when the instance is no longer required. Failure to do so can result in memory leaks such that the application will continue to use up system memory until none is left. Those familiar with Java will be used to relying on the *garbage collector* to free up unused memory automatically. Some implementations of Objective-C also have a garbage collector but it is not implemented on all platforms, notably iOS up to and including iOS 6. Fortunately the iOS 5 SDK introduced Automatic Reference Counting (ARC) which provides a mechanism that avoids the necessity to manually release memory in your code. If you are developing on a platform without ARC implemented, you should get into the practice of releasing allocated memory yourself:

```
[account1 release];
```

If, on the other hand, you are using Xcode 4.2 or later there is no need to manually release objects unless you specifically disable ARC support.

13.10 Calling Methods and Accessing Instance Data

Given the length of this chapter, now is probably a good time to recap what we have done so far. We have now created a new class called *BankAccount*. Within this new class we declared some instance variables to contain the bank account number and current balance together with some instance methods used to set, get and display these values. In the preceding section we covered the steps necessary to create and initialize an instance of our new class. The next step is to learn how to call the instance methods we built into our class.

The syntax for invoking methods is to place the object pointer variable name and method to be called in square brackets ([]). For example, to call the *displayAccountInfo* method on the instance of the class we created previously we would use the following syntax:

```
[account1 displayAccountInfo];
```

When the method accepts a single argument, the method name is followed by a colon (:) followed by the value to be passed to the method. For example, to set the account number:

```
[account1 setAccountNumber: 34543212];
```

In the case of methods taking multiple arguments (as is the case with our *setAccount* method) syntax similar to the following is employed:

```
[account1 setAccount: 4543455 andBalance: 3010.10];
```

13.11 **Creating the Program Section**

The last stage in this exercise is to bring together all the components we have created so that we can actually see the concept working. The last section we need to look at is called the *program section*. This is where we write the code to create the class instance and call the instance methods. Most Objective-C programs have a *main()* routine which is the start point for the application. Based on the selections made when the BankAccount project was created, Xcode has already created a template main() routine contained in the file named *main.m*. Select this file in the Project Navigator panel and modify it as follows, making sure to import the *BankAccount.h* file interface file:

```
#import <Foundation/Foundation.h>
#import "BankAccount.h"

int main(int argc, const char * argv[])
{

    @autoreleasepool {

        // Create variable to point to the class instance
        BankAccount *account1;

        // Allocate memory for instance
        account1 = [BankAccount alloc];
```

```
        // Initialize the instance
        account1 = [account1 init];

        // Set the account balance
        [account1 setAccountBalance: 1500.53];

        // Set the account number
        [account1 setAccountNumber: 34543212];

        // Call the method to display the values of
        // the instance variables
        [account1 displayAccountInfo];

        // Set both account number and balance
        [account1 setAccount: 4543455 andBalance: 3010.10];

        // Output values using the getter methods
        NSLog(@"Number = %ld, Balance = %f",
                    [account1 getAccountNumber],
                    [account1 getAccountBalance]);
    }
    return 0;
}
```

13.12 **Compiling and Running the Program**

In order to test the application in Xcode, simply click on the *Run* button in the toolbar. If you are not using Xcode, the program may be compiled from the command line using the following command:

```
clang -fobjc-arc -framework Foundation BankAccount.m main.m -o bank
```

Once compiled, the *bank* executable can be run:

```
./bank
```

When the program has executed, the following output should appear in the Xcode console (or Terminal window if executed from the command line):

```
2012-11-16 14:44:06.634 t[4287:10b] Account Number 34543212 has a
balance of 1500.530000
2012-11-16 14:44:06.635 t[4287:10b] Number = 4543455, Balance =
3010.100000
```

13.13 Summary

Objective-C is, as the name in part suggests, an object oriented programming language. Object oriented programming advocates an approach whereby the code that comprises an application is structured in the form of re-usable software components (referred to as objects) that can be assembled and re-used to implement the required functionality.

The goal of this chapter has been to introduce the basic concepts of object oriented programming, whilst working through the creation of an example program designed to demonstrate this concept in action within the context of the Objective-C programming language.

14. Writing Objective-C Class Methods

In *An Overview of Objective-C Object Oriented Programming* we looked in detail at creating *instance methods* and mentioned in passing the existence of another type of method known as the *class method*. In this chapter we will look at the subject of class methods in more detail and also work through an example of adding some class methods to an Objective-C class.

14.1 Instance and Class Methods

Before we delve deeper into the subject of class methods it is first important to explain how these differ from instance methods. Instance methods are essentially code routines that perform tasks solely on instances of a class. In our BankAccount example we created instance methods to get and set the bank account number and bank balance instance variables and to display the current values of those variables. Since each instance of the BankAccount class will have its own instance variables containing corresponding instance specific values, these methods clearly only operate at the instance level of the class.

Class methods, on the other hand, work at the class level and are common to all instances of a class. In *An Overview of Objective-C Object Oriented Programming* we talked about how the BankAccount class was derived from the *NSObject* class and, as such, inherited a number of class methods from this parent. In particular the BankAccount class inherited the *alloc* and *init* methods used to allocate memory for, and initialize instances of, the class. Since these methods are specific to the class overall, as opposed to working on different instance data encapsulated in each class instance, they are considered to be *class methods*.

14.2 Creating a New Class Method

In order to demonstrate the concept of class methods we are going to continue to work on the BankAccount class and add a class method that will count the number of instances of the BankAccount class that have been initiated. To do this we are going to write a new *alloc* method named *newAlloc* for a class. The elements we need to achieve this are as follows:

- A static variable accessible to all class instances to store the instance count
- A declaration for a our *newAlloc* class method in the *@interface* section
- A declaration for a class method to return the current value of the instance count in the *@interface* section
- Implementations of the two new class methods in the *@implementation* section
- Some code to create instances of the class using the *newAlloc* method and to obtain and output the instance count

Now that we know what we need to write, we can begin creating our class method example.

14.3 **The @interface Section**

Our interface section needs to declare two class methods. In *An Overview of Objective-C Object Oriented Programming* we learned that instance methods are prefixed by the minus sign (-). We declare class methods using the plus sign (+) as follows in our BankAccount.h file:

```
#import <Foundation/Foundation.h>

@interface BankAccount: NSObject
{
        double accountBalance;
        long accountNumber;
}
-(void) setAccount: (long) y andBalance: (double) x;
-(void) setAccountBalance: (double) x;
-(double) getAccountBalance;
-(void) setAccountNumber: (long) y;
-(long) getAccountNumber;
-(void) displayAccountInfo;
+(BankAccount *) newAlloc;
+(int) totalOpen;
@end
```

We now have our two class methods declared. Note that since the *newAlloc* method is to return a pointer to a block of memory where we will be initializing an instance of a BankAccount class we must declare the return type accordingly. As indicated, the *totalOpen* method will return an integer. Neither method accepts any arguments.

The next step is to work on the implementation of these methods.

14.4 The @implementation Section

The first item needed in the implementation section of our class is a variable to contain the current count of instances. Since we want this variable to be visible only within the scope of this file we will declare the variable as *static* (the topic of variable scope is covered in detail in *Objective-C Variable Scope and Storage Class*). We then need to implement our two new class methods. Let's start by writing the code in our *BankAccount.m* file and then analyze what we are doing:

```
#import "BankAccount.h"


static int openAccounts = 0;


@implementation BankAccount


-(void) setAccount: (long) y andBalance: (double) x;
{

        accountBalance = x;
        accountNumber = y;

}
-(void) setAccountBalance: (double) x
{

        accountBalance = x;

}

-(double) getAccountBalance
{

        return accountBalance;

}
```

```
-(void) setAccountNumber: (long) y
{
        accountNumber = y;
}

-(long) getAccountNumber
{
        return accountNumber;
}

-(void) displayAccountInfo
{
        NSLog (@"Account Number %ld has a balance of %f",
accountNumber, accountBalance);
}

+(BankAccount *) newAlloc
{
        openAccounts++;

        return [BankAccount alloc];
}

+(int) totalOpen
{
        return openAccounts;
}
@end
```

The first line of the implementation creates a static integer variable in which we will store the count of BankAccount instances and initializes it to 0. Within the body of the implementation we then have our *newAlloc* class method. This method increments the current value of the *openAccounts* integer before calling the standard *alloc* class method and returning a pointer to the allocated memory space.

The *totalOpen* class method simply returns the current value of the *openAccounts* variable.

14.5 The main() Function

Now that we have our interface and implementation written, we can modify our *main.m* file to create some instances of the BankAccount class using our *newAlloc* method. The code to do this involves creating some variables to store pointers to the class instances and then calling *newAlloc* and *init*:

```
BankAccount *account1, *account2;
account1 = [[BankAccount newAlloc] init];
account2 = [[BankAccount newAlloc] init];
```

Having created the two instances of the class we can then call the *totalOpen* method to obtain the number of instances:

```
int count = [BankAccount totalOpen];
```

Note that because we are calling a class method, we reference the class in the above code (i.e. BankAccount) and not either of the instances (i.e. account1 and account2).

All together, our *main.m* file should appear as follows:

```
#include "BankAccount.h"

int main (int argc, const char * argv[])
{
    @autoreleasepool {

        BankAccount *account1, *account2;

        account1 = [[BankAccount newAlloc] init];
        account2 = [[BankAccount newAlloc] init];

        int count = [BankAccount totalOpen];

        NSLog (@"Number of BankAccount instances = %i", count);
    }
    return 0;
```

```
}
```

This application can be compiled from within the Xcode environment or from the command line as follows:

```
clang -fobjc-arc -framework Foundation BankAccount.m main.m -o main
```

When executed, we should see output generated as follows:

```
2012-04-15 16:07:07.958 main[2947:10b] Number of BankAccount
instances = 2
```

15. Objective-C - Data Encapsulation, Synthesized Accessors and Dot Notation

In the chapter entitled *An Overview of Objective-C Object Oriented Programming* we looked at the basics of creating and working with objects in Objective-C. In this chapter we will look more closely at accessing data encapsulated in classes through the use of synthesized accessor methods, properties and dot notation.

15.1 Data Encapsulation

In the previous chapters we mentioned briefly the concept of data encapsulation whereby data is contained within objects and is not accessible by any means other than via methods defined in the class. In our BankAccount class example we defined two instance variables and then wrote some methods to get, set and display those values. In this chapter we will look at some alternate programming techniques to access the data encapsulated in a class.

15.2 Properties, Synthesized Accessor Methods

Accessor methods (also referred to as *getters* and *setters*) are methods belonging to a class that allow the programmer to get and set the values of instance variables contained within that class. The BankAccount example covered in the previous chapters we wrote accessor methods to get and set the bank account number and bank balance variables. As you can probably imagine, having to write these methods for large numbers of complex classes will ultimately prove to be time consuming. Fortunately, Objective-C provides a mechanism that automates the creation of accessor methods. These are called *synthesized accessor methods* and are implemented through the use of the *@property* directive. The following code demonstrates a modified version of our BankAccount class *interface* definition file with the two getters and setters we originally wrote removed and the two instance variables declared as properties via the *@property* directive. Note also the removal of the braces ({}) around the instance variables when they are declared as properties:

```
#import <Foundation/Foundation.h>
```

```
@interface BankAccount: NSObject
@property double accountBalance;
@property long accountNumber;
-(void) setAccount: (long) y andBalance: (double) x;
-(void) displayAccountInfo;
+(BankAccount *) newAlloc;
+(int) totalOpen;
@end
```

Note also that because the two properties are of different data types (double and long) it was necessary to declare them on separate *@property* lines. Had they been of the same data type we could have placed them on the same line, separated by commas:

```
@property int x, y;
```

Having created the properties, the question that now arises is what the synthesized accessor methods will be named when they are generated by the compiler.

In assigning a name to a synthesized accessor setter method, Objective-C takes the name of the instance variable (for example *accountBalance*), capitalizes the first letter (*AccountBalance*) and then pre-fixes it with *set* (*setAccountBalance*). For example:

```
BankAccount *account1;
account1 = [[BankAccount alloc] init];
[account1 setAccountBalance: 1500.53];
[account1 setAccountNumber: 34543212];
```

In the case of the getter method, this simply adopts the name of the property. For example, the getter method name for the *accountNumber* property is also *accountNumber*:

```
long myAccount = [account1 accountNumber];
```

15.3 Accessing Property Instance Variables

As we have seen, the properties of a class instance can be accessed using synthesized accessor methods. It is also generally necessary to access properties from within the instance methods of the class. Take, for example, the code for our *displayAccountInfo* instance method:

```
-(void) displayAccountInfo
{
        NSLog (@"Account Number %ld has a balance of %f",
          accountNumber, accountBalance);
}
```

With the two instance variables wrapped in properties, the above code will fail to compile with an error stating that the accountNumber and accountBalance variables are undefined. The reason for this is that when using properties, the underlying instance variable is synthesized using the instance variable name prefixed with an underscore. For example:

```
-(void) displayAccountInfo
{
        NSLog (@"Account Number %ld has a balance of %f",
          _accountNumber, _accountBalance);
}
```

15.4 The Modified Bank Account Example

The code for the example BankAccount application, after being adapted to use properties and synthesized accessors, now reads as follows:

BankAccount.h:

```
#import <Foundation/Foundation.h>

@interface BankAccount : NSObject
@property double accountBalance;
@property long accountNumber;

-(void) setAccount: (long) y andBalance: (double) x;
-(void) displayAccountInfo;
+(BankAccount *) newAlloc;
+(int) totalOpen;
```

```
@end
```

BankAccount.m:

```
#import "BankAccount.h"

static int openAccounts = 0;

@implementation BankAccount
-(void) setAccount: (long) y andBalance: (double) x;
{
        _accountBalance = x;
        _accountNumber = y;
}

-(void) displayAccountInfo
{
        NSLog (@"Account Number %ld has a balance of %f",
          _accountNumber, _accountBalance);
}

+(BankAccount *) newAlloc
{
        openAccounts++;

        return [BankAccount alloc];
}

+(int) totalOpen
{
        return openAccounts;
}
@end
```

main.m:

```
#import <Foundation/Foundation.h>
```

```
#import "BankAccount.h"

int main(int argc, const char * argv[])
{
    @autoreleasepool {
      BankAccount *account1;

      account1 = [BankAccount alloc];
      account1 = [account1 init];
      [account1 setAccountBalance: 1500.53];
      [account1 setAccountNumber: 34543212];

      [account1 displayAccountInfo];

      [account1 setAccount: 4543455 andBalance: 3010.10];

      NSLog(@"Number = %ld, Balance = %f",
               [account1 accountNumber],
               [account1 accountBalance]);
    }
    return 0;
}
```

The true power of properties is most noticeable in the *BankAccount.m* implementation file where the use of properties has reduced the number of methods that needed to be implemented from six down to four.

15.5 Objective-C and Dot Notation

Those familiar with object oriented programming in Java, C++ or C# are probably reeling a little from the syntax used in Objective-C. They are probably thinking life was much easier when they could just use something called *dot notation* to set and get the values of instance variables. The good news is that one of the features introduced into version 2.0 of Objective-C is support for dot notation.

Dot notation involves accessing an instance variable by specifying a class instance followed by a dot followed in turn by the name of the instance variable or property to be accessed:

```
classinstance.property
```

For example, to get the current value of our *accountBalance* instance variable:

```
double balance1 = account1.accountBalance;
```

Dot notation can also be used to set values of instance properties:

```
account1.accountBalance = 6789.98;
```

A key point to understand about dot notation is that it only works for instance variables for which synthesized accessor methods have been declared. An attempt to use dot notation to access an instance variable for which no synthesized accessor is available will result in the code failing to compile with an error similar to:

```
error: request for member 'accountBalance' in something not a
structure or union
```

15.6 **Summary**

Data encapsulation involves the enclosure of data members within a class whereby access to that data is controlled through the methods of that class. When using instance variables, it was necessary to manually write getter and setter accessor methods to allow access to encapsulated instance variables. By wrapping those instance variables in properties, however, the compiler can be used to automatically synthesize these accessor methods for us thereby saving considerable programming time and effort.

This chapter has also covered the concept of using dot notation to access the data elements of a class instance, a concept that will be familiar to those used to programming in languages such as C++, C# or Java.

16. Objective-C Inheritance

In the *An Overview of Objective-C Object Oriented Programming* chapter, we covered the basic concepts of object-oriented programming and worked through an example of creating a new class using Objective-C. In that example, our new class was derived from the NSObject base class and, as such, inherited a number of traits from that parent class. In this chapter we will explore the subject of inheritance in greater detail.

16.1 Inheritance, Classes and Subclasses

The concept of inheritance brings something of a real-world view to programming. It allows a class to be defined that has a certain set of characteristics (such as methods and instance variables) and then other classes to be created which are derived from that class. The derived class inherits all of the features of the parent class and typically then adds some features of its own.

By deriving classes we create what is often referred to as a *class hierarchy*. The class at the top of the hierarchy is known as the *base class* or *root class* and the derived classes as *subclasses* or *child classes*. Any number of subclasses may be derived from a class. The class from which a subclass is derived is called the *parent class* or *super class*.

Classes need not only be derived from a root class. For example, a subclass can also inherit from another subclass with the potential to create large and complex class hierarchies.

In Objective-C a subclass can only be derived from a single direct parent class. This is a concept referred to as *single inheritance*.

16.2 An Objective-C Inheritance Example

As with most programming concepts, the subject of inheritance in Objective-C is perhaps best illustrated with an example. In *An Overview of Objective-C Object Oriented Programming* we created a class named *BankAccount* designed to hold a bank account number and corresponding current balance. In the chapter entitled *Objective-C - Data*

Objective-C Inheritance

Encapsulation, Synthesized Accessors and Dot Notation, this example was modified to use properties and synthesized accessor methods.

The BankAccount class contained both instance variables and instance methods. The interface and implementation declarations for this class are reproduced below.

BankAccount.h:

```
#import <Foundation/Foundation.h>

@interface BankAccount : NSObject
@property double accountBalance;
@property long accountNumber;


-(void) setAccount: (long) y andBalance: (double) x;
-(void) displayAccountInfo;
+(BankAccount *) newAlloc;
+(int) totalOpen;
@end
```

BankAccount.m

```
#import "BankAccount.h"

static int openAccounts = 0;

@implementation BankAccount
-(void) setAccount: (long) y andBalance: (double) x;
{
        _accountBalance = x;
        _accountNumber = y;
}


-(void) displayAccountInfo
{
        NSLog (@"Account Number %ld has a balance of %f",
          _accountNumber, _accountBalance);
```

```
}

+(BankAccount *) newAlloc
{
        openAccounts++;

        return [BankAccount alloc];
}

+(int) totalOpen
{
        return openAccounts;
}
@end
```

As we can see from the declaration, this class is a subclass of the NSObject base class and contains a number of properties and instance methods. Though this is a somewhat basic class it does everything necessary if all you need it to do is store an account number and account balance. Suppose, however, that in addition to the BankAccount class you also needed a class to be used for savings accounts. A savings account will still need to hold an account number and a current balance and methods will still be needed to access that data. One option would be to create an entirely new class, one that duplicates all of the functionality of the BankAccount class together with the new features required by a savings account. A more efficient approach, however, would be to create a new class that is a *subclass* of the BankAccount class. The new class will then inherit all the features of the BankAccount class, but can then be extended to add the additional functionality required by a savings account.

To create a subclass of BankAccount that we will call SavingsAccount, we simply write the appropriate interface and implementation structure, this time specifying BankAccount instead of NSObject as the parent class (inheritance passes down through all levels of the class hierarchy so SavingsAccount will still inherit from NSObject via the BankAccount parent class).

16.3 **Modifying the BankAccount Project**

Launch Xcode and open the BankAccount project. The first step is to add the files for the new class. To achieve this, Ctrl-click on the *BankAccount* entry located at the top of the Project Navigator panel and select *New File…* from the menu. Alternatively, select *File -> New -> File…* from the Xcode menu bar at the top of the screen. Within the new file panel, select *Objective-C class* and click *Next*. On the options panel, name the new class *SavingsAccount* and enter *BankAccount* into the *Subclass of* field.

Select and review the newly created *SavingsAccount.h* file in the Project Navigator panel:

```
#import "BankAccount.h"

@interface SavingsAccount : BankAccount

@end
```

Note that although we have yet to add any instance variables or methods, the class has actually inherited all the methods and variables of the parent BankAccount class. We could, therefore, create an instance of the SavingsAccount class and set variables and call methods in exactly the same way we did with the BankAccount class in previous examples. That said, we haven't really achieved anything unless we actually take steps to extend the class.

16.4 **Extending the Functionality of a Subclass**

So far we have been able to create a subclass that contains all the functionality of the parent class (including the functionality the parent class inherited from its parent class and so on). In order for this exercise to make sense, however, we now need to extend the subclass so that it has the features we need to make it useful for storing savings account information. To do this, we simply add the properties and methods that provide the new functionality, just as we would for any other class we might wish to create:

```
#import "BankAccount.h"

@interface SavingsAccount : BankAccount
@property float interestRate;
-(float) calculateInterest;
```

```
@end
```

Having declared the property and method for the interest rate, the next step is to implement the *calculateInterest* method in the *SavingsAccount.m* implementation file. Select this file in the Project Navigator panel, therefore, and modify it as follows:

```
#import "SavingsAccount.h"

@implementation SavingsAccount

-(float) calculateInterest
{
      return _interestRate * self.accountBalance;
}
@end
```

Note that although the instance variable assigned to the interestRate property can be accessed using the synthesized *_interestRate* name, we have used dot notation to access the *accountBalance* property of something called *self*:

```
self.accountBalance
```

The reason for this is that the accountBalance property is not a member of the SavingsAccount class, but rather an inherited member of the BankAccount superclass. In order for the compiler to identify where this property resides, we have to specifically tell it that it belongs to the current class. This can be achieved by using the *self* keyword, which simply refers to the current class instance. As an alternative, we could also have referred to the superclass when referencing the variable using the *super* keyword:

```
super.accountBalance
```

Note that the use of dot notation in this context is simply a stylistic choice. The same result could have been achieved by calling the *accountBalance* accessor method of the class:

```
[self accountBalance];
```

With these changes made we have a class that inherits the features of the BankAccount class but now has an additional property in the form of *interestRate* and a new method named *calculateInterest*. The rest of the functionality we needed we essentially got for free by inheriting from the BankAccount class.

16.5 **Overriding Inherited Methods**

When using inheritance it is not unusual to find a method in the parent class that almost does what you need, but requires modification to provide the precise functionality required. That said, it is also possible you'll inherit a method with a name that describes exactly what you want to do, but it actually does not come close to doing what you need. One option in this scenario would be to ignore the inherited method and write a new method with an entirely new name. A better option is to *override* the inherited method and write a new version of it in the subclass.

Before proceeding with an example, there are two rules that must be obeyed when overriding a method. Firstly, the overriding method in the subclass must take exactly the same number and type of arguments as the overridden method in the parent class. Secondly, the new method must have the same return type as the parent method.

In our BankAccount class we have a method named *displayAccountInfo* which displays the bank account number and current balance held by an instance of the class. In our SavingsAccount subclass we might also want to output the current interest rate assigned to the account. To achieve this, we simply declare a new version of the *displayAccountInfo* method in our SavingsAccount subclass:

```
#import "SavingsAccount.h"


@implementation SavingsAccount


-(float) calculateInterest
{
        return _interestRate * super.accountBalance;
}


-(void) displayAccountInfo
{
```

```
        NSLog (@"Account Number %ld has a balance of %f and is
earning %f interest", self.accountNumber, self.accountBalance,
_interestRate);
}
@end
```

Now that we have completed work on our SavingsAccount class we can modify the code in *main.m* to create an instance and start manipulating the object using our inherited, overridden and subclass specific methods:

```
#import <Foundation/Foundation.h>
#import "BankAccount.h"
#import "SavingsAccount.h"

int main(int argc, const char * argv[])
{

    @autoreleasepool {
        SavingsAccount *account1 = [[SavingsAccount alloc] init];
        [account1 setAccount: 4543455 andBalance: 3010.10];
        [account1 setInterestRate: 0.001];

        float interestEarned = [account1 calculateInterest];

        NSLog (@"Interest earned = %f", interestEarned);

        [account1 displayAccountInfo];

    }
    return 0;
}
```

16.6 Testing the Program

Test that the code works by clicking on the *Run* button in the Xcode toolbar. If you are not using Xcode, compile the code from the command line using the following command:

```
clang -fobjc-arc -framework Foundation BankAccount.m SavingsAccount.m
main.m -o bank
```

Once executed, the output from the code should read as follows:

```
2012-11-16 16:37:33.724 bank[36074:707] Interest earned = 3.010100
2012-11-16 16:37:33.726 bank[36074:707] Account Number 4543455 has a
balance of 3010.100000 and is earning 0.001000 interest
```

16.7 **Summary**

Inheritance extends the concept of object re-use in object oriented programming by allowing new classes to be derived from existing classes, and those new classes subsequently extended to add new functionality. When an existing class provides some, but not all, of the functionality required by the programmer, inheritance allows that class to be used as the basis for a new subclass. The new subclass will inherit all the capabilities of the parent class, but may then be extended to add the missing functionality.

17. Pointers and Indirection in Objective-C

In the preceding chapters on object-oriented programming we have used, but not described, a feature of Objective-C (actually derived from the underlying C programming language) in the form of *pointers* and *indirection*. A clear understanding of this topic is important when working with objects and also when passing values as arguments to methods and functions.

17.1 How Variables are Stored

When we declare a variable in Objective-C and assign a value to it we are essentially allocating a location in memory where that value is stored. Take, for example, the following variable declaration:

```
int myvar = 10;
```

When the above code is executed, a block of memory large enough to hold an integer value is reserved in memory and the value of 10 is placed at that location. Whenever we reference this variable in code, we are actually using the variable value. For example, the following code adds the value of *myvar* (i.e. 10) to the constant value 20 to arrive at a result of 30.

```
int result = 20 + myvar;
```

Similarly, when we pass a variable through as an argument to a method or function we are actually passing the *value* of the variable, not the variable itself. To better understand this concept, consider the following sample program:

```
#import <Foundation/Foundation.h>

void myFunction(int i)
{
```

```
        i = i + 10;
}


int main (int argc, const char * argv[])
{
    @autoreleasepool {

        int myvar = 10;

        NSLog (@"Before call to function myvar = %i", myvar);
        myFunction (myvar);
        NSLog (@"After call to function myvar = %i", myvar);
    }
    return 0;
}
```

The above program consists of a main function that declares our *myvar* variable and displays the current value. It then calls the function *myFunction* passing through the value of the *myvar* variable. The *myFunction* function adds 10 to the value it was passed as an argument and then returns to the main function where the value of *myvar* is once again displayed. When compiled and executed the following output is displayed:

```
Before call to function myvar = 10
After call to function myvar = 10
```

Clearly, even though the value passed through to *myFunction* was increased by 10, the value of *myvar* remained unchanged. This is because what was passed through as an argument to *myFunction* was the *value* of *myvar*, not the *myvar* variable itself. Therefore, in *myFunction* we were simply working on a constant value of 10 that had absolutely no connection to the original *myvar* variable.

In order to be able to work on the actual variable in the function we need to use something called indirection.

17.2 **An Overview of Indirection**

Indirection involves working with pointers to the location of variables and objects rather than the contents of those items. In other words, instead of working with the *value* stored in a variable, we work with a *pointer* to the *memory address* where the variable is located.

Pointers are declared by prefixing the name with an asterisk (*) character. For example, to declare a pointer to our *myvar* variable we would write the following code:

```
int myvar = 10;
int *myptr;
```

In the above example we have declared our *myvar* variable and then declared a variable named *myptr* as being of type *pointer to an integer*. Having declared both our variable and our pointer we now need to assign the *address* of our variable to the pointer. The address of a variable is referenced by prefixing it with the ampersand (&) character. We can, therefore, extend our example to assign the address of the *myvar* variable to the *myptr* variable:

```
int myvar = 10;
int *myptr;


myptr = &myvar;
```

We have now implemented a level of indirection by creating a *pointer* to our variable. As such, we can now pass this pointer through as an argument to our function such that we will be able to work on the actual variable, rather than just the value (10) of the variable. In order to access the value of a variable using a pointer to that variable, we prefix the pointer variable name with an asterisk (*). When we do this, we are telling the compiler we want to work with the contents of the variable or object at the memory address contained within the pointer:

```
int myvar = 10;
int *myptr;


myptr = &myvar;


*myptr = *myptr + 15;
```

Similarly, we can modify our function to accept a pointer to an integer and perform the addition on that variable. As such, we can now modify our previous program as follows:

```
#import <Foundation/Foundation.h>

void myFunction(int *i)
{
        *i = *i + 10;
}

int main (int argc, const char * argv[])
{
    @autoreleasepool {

        int myvar = 10;
        int *myptr;

        myptr = &myvar;
        NSLog (@"Before call to function myvar = %i", myvar);
        myFunction (myptr);
        NSLog (@"After call to function myvar = %i", myvar);
    }
    return 0;
}
```

Now because we are passing through a pointer to *myvar* when we call the function and have modified the function to work with the contents of the variable, the output clearly indicates that the function changed the value of *myvar* when it was called. We have, therefore, just used indirection.

```
Before call to function myvar = 10
After call to function myvar = 20
```

17.3 **Indirection and Objects**

So far in this chapter we have used indirection with a variable. The same concept applies for objects. In previous chapters we worked with our BankAccount class. When doing so we wrote statements similar to the following:

```
BankAccount *account1;
BankAccount *account1 = [[BankAccount alloc] init];
```

The first line of code (BankAccount *account1;) is actually declaring that the variable named *account1* is a *pointer to an object of type BankAccount*. We are, therefore, using indirection to provide a handle to our object. The calls to the *alloc* and *init* methods subsequently create the object in memory and the assign the address of that object to the *account1* pointer variable. We are, therefore, using indirection once again.

One key point to note is that we do not need to prefix the object pointer with a * when performing operations such as calling methods. For example, we can call a method on our *account1* object without using an asterisk:

```
[account1 displayAccountInfo];
```

17.4 **Indirection and Object Copying**

Due to the fact that references to objects utilize indirection, it is important to understand that when we use the assignment operator (=) to assign one object to another we are not actually creating a copy of the object. Instead, we are creating a copy of the pointer to the object. Consider, therefore, the following code:

```
BankAccount *account1;
BankAccount *account2;

BankAccount *account1 = [[BankAccount alloc] init];

account2 = account1;
```

In the above example, we will end up with two pointers (*account1* and *account2*) that point to the same location in memory. We have not, therefore, created a copy of *account1*. For details on copying objects refer to *Copying Objects in Objective-C*.

17.5 **Summary**

When working with variables and objects in Objective-C it is important to have a clear understanding of the way in which these items are stored in memory and subsequently accessed in code. This is of particular importance when passing references to variables or objects from one function or method to another.

18. Objective-C Dynamic Binding and Typing with the id Type

So far in this series of chapters covering object oriented programming with Objective-C we have focused exclusively on static class typing and binding. In this chapter we will look at concepts referred to as *dynamic typing* and *dynamic binding* and explore how the Objective-C *id* type is used in this context.

18.1 Static Typing vs. Dynamic Typing

In previous chapters, when we have created an instance of a class we have done so by specifically declaring the type of object we are creating. For example, when we created an instance of our BankAccount class, we created a variable of type *BankAccount* to store a reference to the instance object:

```
BankAccount *account1;
account1 = [[BankAccount alloc] init];
```

Because we have pre-declared the type of object that is to be assigned to the *account1* variable we have performed something called *static typing*. This is also sometimes referred to as *compile time* typing because we have provided enough information for the compiler to check for errors during the compilation process.

Often when writing object oriented code we won't always know in advance what type of object might need to be assigned to a variable. This is particularly true when passing objects through as arguments to functions or methods. It is much easier to write a single, general purpose function or method that can handle an object from any class, than to write a different function or method for each class in an application. This is where the concept of *dynamic typing* is used. Dynamic typing allows us to declare a variable that is capable of storing any type of object, regardless of its class origins. This is achieved using the Objective-C *id* type. The *id* type is a special, general purpose data type that can be assigned an object of any type.

In the following dynamic typing example, we create a variable of type *id* named *object1* and then assign a *BankAccount* object to it. We then call a method on the object before releasing it. We then use the same object1 variable to store an object of type *CustomerInfo* and call a method on that object:

```
id object1;

object1 = [[SavingsAccount alloc] init];

[object1 setAccount: 4543455 andBalance: 3010.10];

object1 = [[CustomerInfo alloc] init];

[object1 displayInfo];
```

18.2 **Dynamic Binding**

Dynamic typing is about using the *id* type to provide a variable that can be used to store objects of any type during program execution. *Dynamic binding* takes this concept one step further by allowing methods on an object stored in an *id* variable to be called without prior knowledge of the type of object currently assigned to the variable.

Suppose, for example, that we want to write a function that is passed an object. Within the function the *displayInfo* method of that object is called. Without dynamic typing and dynamic binding we would need to write one function for each class type that we wanted to be able to handle. With Objective-C's dynamic typing and binding we can declare the object argument as being type *id*, thereby allowing us to pass any object through to the function. Secondly, we can then rely on dynamic binding to ensure that when we call the object's *displayInfo* method within the function, we are calling it on the correct object (i.e. the one that was passed through as an argument).

Let's begin by writing our function:

```
void objDisplay (id object)
{
        [object displayInfo];
}
```

As we can see from the above code, the function is called *objDisplay*, it accepts an object as the single argument which is assigned to an *id* type variable, and then makes a call to the *displayInfo* method of the object. We can now combine this function with a main routine that creates two different object types and then calls the *objDisplay* function for each:

```
int main (int argc, const char * argv[])
{
    @autoreleasepool {
        id object1;

        object1 = [[SavingsAccount alloc] init];

        [object1 setAccount: 4543455 andBalance: 3010.10];

        objDisplay (object1);

        object1 = [[CustomerInfo alloc] init];

        objDisplay (object1);
    }
    return 0;
}
```

Note that the *objDisplay* function makes the assumption that the object it has been passed actually has a method named *displayInfo*. This highlights a shortcoming of dynamic typing and binding in that the compiler will be unable to warn you of any errors such as attempting to call a non-existent method on a dynamically typed object variable. The problem will only become apparent when the program is running. If, for example, the *CustomerInfo* class lacked a *displayInfo* method, the program would terminate in the *objDisplay* method with an error similar to:

```
*** Terminating app due to uncaught exception
'NSInvalidArgumentException', reason: '***
-[CustomerInfo displayAccountInfo]: unrecognized selector sent to
instance 0x104cc0'
```

This brings us to the subject of *polymorphism*.

18.3 **Polymorphism**

Polymorphism is the ability to have methods with the same name in different classes. For example both our *SavingsAccount* and *CustomerInfo* classes in the above examples have *displayInfo* methods. Whilst the code and resulting output displayed is different for each method they both ultimately achieve the same result (i.e. displaying the values assigned to the encapsulated instance variables). Polymorphism is a key concept in providing a consistent programming interface to the classes you create in your program. If all the classes have a method that performs a similar task then programming convention dictates that they should be given the same names. This helps both in writing code to work with objects and also with the use of dynamic binding.

18.4 **Summary**

Sometimes when developing using Objective-C it is not always possible to know in advance what type of object might need to be assigned to a variable, particularly when passing objects through as arguments to functions or methods. This is where the concept of *dynamic typing* and the *id* type is used. Dynamic typing allows us to declare a variable that is capable of storing any type of object, regardless of its class origins. The *id* type is a special, general purpose data type that can be used to reference an object of any type.

19. Objective-C Variable Scope and Storage Class

In previous chapters we have invested a considerable amount of time talking about variables in terms of the various types available and how they are defined. One area we have yet to cover involves the places from which a variable is accessible once it has been declared. This is a concept known as *variable scope* and the scope of a variable is very much dependent upon where it is declared within the Objective-C code of a program.

In this chapter we will also look at the Objective-C variable storage classes. These are specifiers that tell the Objective-C compiler information about how the variable is going to be used within the application code.

19.1 **Variable Scope**

An Objective-C program will consist of code divided up into functions, classes, methods and code structures (such as *do ... while* and *for* loops). Invariably a typical program will make extensive use of variables to store and manipulate data. Once a variable has been declared, it may or may not be accessible to other sections of the program code. This accessibility depends on where and how the variable was declared and where the code is that needs to access it. This is known as *variable scope* and falls into a number of categories, each of which will be covered in this chapter.

19.2 **Block Scope**

Objective-C code is divided into sequences of code blocks and files that define the structure of a program. Each block, referred to as a *statement block*, is encapsulated by braces ({}). For example, a *for* loop typically contains a statement block:

```
int x;

for (x = 0; x < 10; x++)
{
```

```
    int j = x + 10;
    NSLog (@"j = %i", j);
}
```

In the above example, variable *j* is declared within the statement block of the *for* loop and as such is considered to be *local* to that block. This means that the variable can be accessed from within the *for* loop statement block but is essentially invisible and inaccessible to code anywhere else in the program code. Any attempt to access variable *j* outside the *for* loop will result in a compile error. For example:

```
int x;

for (x = 0; x < 10; x++)
{
    int j = x + 10;
    NSLog (@"j = %i", j);
}

j += 20; // illegal - j is now out of scope
```

An attempt to compile the above code within the context of an application will result in a compilation error along the lines of the following:

```
error: use of undeclared identifier 'j'
```

An interesting side effect of variable scope within this context is that it enables us to have more than one variable with the same name as long as they are in different scopes. For example, we can have a variable named *j* declared outside the *for* loop and a variable named *j* declared inside the *for* loop. Although these variables have the same name they occupy different memory locations and contain different values. This can be illustrated using a simple application that contains two *j* variables:

```
#import <Foundation/Foundation.h>

int main (int argc, const char * argv[])
{
    @autoreleasepool {
```

```
        int x;
        int j = 54321;

        for (x = 0; x < 10; x++)
        {
                int j = x + 10;
                NSLog (@"Variable j in for loop is %i", j);
        }

        NSLog (@"Variable j outside for loop is %i", j);
    }
    return 0;
}
```

As we can see from the above code, variable *j* is declared twice but in two different scopes. When compiled and executed we can see that modifying the value of *j* within the *for* loop has no effect on the value assigned to the variable *j* declared outside the for loop:

```
2009-10-19 15:09:39.875 t[8130:10b] Variable j in for loop is 10
2009-10-19 15:09:39.877 t[8130:10b] Variable j in for loop is 11
2009-10-19 15:09:39.877 t[8130:10b] Variable j in for loop is 12
2009-10-19 15:09:39.878 t[8130:10b] Variable j in for loop is 13
2009-10-19 15:09:39.878 t[8130:10b] Variable j in for loop is 14
2009-10-19 15:09:39.879 t[8130:10b] Variable j in for loop is 15
2009-10-19 15:09:39.879 t[8130:10b] Variable j in for loop is 16
2009-10-19 15:09:39.879 t[8130:10b] Variable j in for loop is 17
2009-10-19 15:09:39.880 t[8130:10b] Variable j in for loop is 18
2009-10-19 15:09:39.880 t[8130:10b] Variable j in for loop is 19
2009-10-19 15:09:39.881 t[8130:10b] Variable j outside for loop is
54321
```

19.3 Function Scope

Objective-C code is typically structured into a number of classes and code units called *functions* and *methods* (for more details on functions see *An Overview of Objective-C Functions*). In terms of variable scope, functions and methods are really little more than statement blocks in that they are encapsulated in braces, and variables declared within those braces are *local* to that block.

The following example is intended to illustrate this concept and contains two functions named *main()* and *multiply()* respectively.

```objc
#import <Foundation/Foundation.h>


int main (int argc, const char * argv[])
{
    @autoreleasepool {

        int j = 10;
        int k = 20;
        int result;

        result = multiply();

    }
    return 0;
}

int multiply()
{
        return j * k;
}
```

An attempt to compile the above code example will result in a compiler error similar to the following:

```
In function 'multiply':
error: 'j' undeclared (first use in this function)
error: (Each undeclared identifier is reported only once
error: for each function it appears in.)
error: 'k' undeclared (first use in this function)
```

The reason for this error is that variables *j* and *k* are declared in the *main()* function and are, therefore, local to that function. As such, these variables are not visible to the *multiply()* function, thereby resulting in an error when we try to reference them. If we wanted to have access to the values of those variables we would have to pass them through as arguments to the multiply function (for details on function arguments refer to *An Overview of Objective-C Functions*) or specify them as global or static variables (discussed below).

As with block scope, it is possible to have multiple variables with the same name inside a single function as long as each instance appears within its own local scope. For example, we can add a *while* loop to our *main()* that has its own local variable also named *j*:

```
int main (int argc, const char * arqv[])
{
    @autoreleasepool {

        int j = 10;
        int k = 20;
        int result;

        while (k > 0)
        {
            int j = 0;
            j += k;
            k--;

        }
    }
    return 0;

}
```

19.4 Global Scope

A variable that has *global scope* is potentially accessible to code anywhere else in an Objective-C program, regardless of whether the code is in a separate file to the one in which the variable is declared. Global variables are declared *outside* of any statement blocks and are typically placed near the top of a source file.

The following is a code listing from an Objective-C source file named *main.m*:

```
#import <Foundation/Foundation.h>


int myVar = 321;


int main (int argc, const char * argv[])
{
    @autoreleasepool {

        NSLog (@"myVar = %i", myVar);
    }
    return 0;
}
```

As we can see, the global variable *myVar* is declared outside of the *main()* function and is not embedded into a statement block or class declaration of any kind. Because this is a global variable, it is directly accessible inside the main function and would also be accessible from any other functions and statement blocks within the context of the *main.m* code file.

As previously stated, global variables are potentially accessible across all the source files that constitute an Objective-C program. The key word here is *potentially*, and we say this because global access across multiple source files is not the default for a global variable. Take, for example, the following two code files. The first file, *main.m* contains the declaration of the global variable *myVar* and calls a function named *displayit()*:

```
#import <Foundation/Foundation.h>

int myVar = 321;
void displayit();

int main (int argc, const char * argv[])
{
    @autoreleasepool {
        NSLog (@"myVar = %i", myVar);
        displayit();
```

```
    }
    return 0;
}
```

The second file, named *displayit.m* contains the code for the *displayit()* function and displays the value currently assigned to the global *myVar* variable:

```
#import <Foundation/Foundation.h>

void displayit()
{
        NSLog (@"MyVar from different source file is %i", myVar);
}
```

If we try to compile these two code files into an executable, either using Xcode or from the command-line, we will get an error that reads as follows:

```
clang -objc-arc -framework Foundation main.m displayit.m -o main
displayit.m:7:59: error: use of undeclared identifier 'myVar'
        NSLog (@"MyVar from different source file is %i", myVar);
                                                          ^
1 error generated.
```

The reason for this is that although the variable was declared as global in *main.m* we still need to take one extra step in *displayit.m* to make the variable accessible in this file. This step involves declaring that the variable is *external* to the local file. This declaration is achieved using the *extern* specifier keyword. For example, to make *myVar* accessible in *displayit.m* the following code would be required:

```
extern int myVar;

void displayit()
{
        NSLog (@"MyVar from different source file is %i", myVar);
}
```

Having made this change, the code will now compile and run.

19.5 **File Scope**

In the preceding section on *global scope* we talked about how a variable declared outside of any statement blocks is considered to be global and may be accessed both by code in the same file, or by code in different files. Suppose, however, that you wanted a variable to be accessible *only* to code within the file where the variable is declared. This is achieved by using the *static* specifier when declaring the variable. For example, the following code is from a file named *main.m*. This file declares variable *myVar* to be static. As such, the variable will be accessible only to code within the *main.m* file and cannot be accessed by code in any other file:

```
#import <Foundation/Foundation.h>


static int myVar = 543;
void displayit();

int main (int argc, const char * argv[])
{
    @autoreleasepool {

        NSLog (@"myVar = %i", myVar);

        displayit();
    }
    return 0;
}
```

19.6 **Variable Storage Class**

Variable storage class specifiers are used when declaring a variable to give the compiler information about how a variable is likely to be used and accessed within the program being compiled. So far in this chapter we have actually already looked at two storage class specifiers in the form of *extern* and *static*. A full list of variable storage class specifiers supported by Objective-C is as follows:

- **extern** - Specifies that the variable name is referencing a global variable specified in a different source file to the current file.

- **static** - Specifies that the variable is to be accessible only within the scope of the current source file.
- **auto** - The default value for variable declarations. Specifies the variable is to be local or global depending on where the declaration is made within the code. Since this is the default setting this specifier is rarely, if ever, used.
- **const** - Declares a variable as being read-only. In other words, specifies that once the variable has been assigned a value, that value will not be subsequently changed.
- **volatile** - Specifies that the value assigned to a variable will be changed in subsequent code. This is the default behavior for variable declarations.

19.7 **Summary**

The location in code, combined with the way in which a variable is declared, governs whether or not that variable is accessible from other areas of code that make up an Objective-C application. This is a concept referred to as *variable scope*.

A variable declared within the statement block of a *for* loop, for example, is *local* to that block and not accessible to code outside of the loop. A variable declared outside of any statement blocks, however, is considered to be global and accessible from anywhere in the same source code file in which it is declared. Global variables are also accessible from other source files as long as the *extern* directive is used to notify the compiler that the variable resides in a different source file. The *static* keyword can be used to confine the scope of a global variable to the file in which it is declared.

Chapter 20

20. An Overview of Objective-C Functions

Functions are a vital part of writing well structured and efficient code. Objective-C functions provide a way to organize programs and avoid code repetition. In this chapter of *Objective-C 2.0 Essentials* we will look at how functions are declared and used.

20.1 What is a Function?

A function is a named block of code that can be called upon to perform a specific task. It can be provided data on which to perform the task and is capable of returning a result to the code that called it. For example, if a particular arithmetic calculation needs to be performed in an Objective-C program, the code to perform the arithmetic can be placed in a function. The function can be programmed to accept the values on which the arithmetic is to be performed (referred to as *arguments*) and to return the result of the calculation. At any point in the program code where the calculation is required, the function is simply called and the result returned.

20.2 How to Declare an Objective-C Function

An Objective-C function is declared using the following syntax:

```
<return type> <function name> (<arg1 type> <arg1 name>, <arg2 type>
<arg2 name>, ... )
{
// Function code
}
```

Explanations of the various fields of the function declaration are as follows:

- **<return type>** - Specifies the data type of the result returned by the function. If the function does not return a result then *void* should be specified. Unless otherwise specified, functions are assumed to return an *int*.
- **<function name>** - The name assigned to the function. This is the name by which the function will be referenced when it is called from within the application code. Note

that, unless otherwise specified using the *static* specifier, function names are global and must be unique within the context of an application to avoid compilation errors.

- **<argn type>** - The type of the argument passed through to the function.
- **<argn name>** - The name by which the argument is to be referenced in the function code.
- **Function code** - The code of the function that does the work.

As an example, the following function takes no arguments, returns no result and simply displays a message:

```
void sayhello ()
{
    NSLog (@"Hello");
}
```

The following sample function, on the other hand, takes two integer arguments and returns the result of a multiplication of those numbers:

```
int multiply (int x, int y)
{
    return x * y;
}
```

20.3 **The main() Function**

If you have been reading this book sequentially, you will have noticed that many of the examples in previous chapters have contained a function called *main*. This is a special function name that tells the Objective-C compiler where program execution is to start when the code is executed. If you do not have a main function your code will fail during the link phase of the build process. The syntax for a main function is as follows:

```
int main (int argc, const char * argv[])
{
    @autoreleasepool {
        // Code here
    }
    return 0;
```

```
}
```

The *argc* argument contains a count of the number of arguments that were found on the command line when the program was executed, and *argv* is a pointer to an array containing those arguments.

20.4 **Calling an Objective-C Function**

Once declared, functions are called using the following syntax:

```
<function name> (<arg1>, <arg2>, ... )
```

For example, to call a function named *sayHello* that takes no arguments and returns no value, we would write the following code:

```
sayhello();
```

To call a function named *multiply* that takes two arguments and returns an integer, on the other hand, we might write the following code:

```
int result;
result = multiply (10, 20);
```

In the above example, we have created a new variable called *result* and then used the assignment operator (=) to store the result returned by the multiply function when it is passed the numbers 10 and 20 as arguments.

Once a function is declared it can be called from anywhere in the code, regardless of whether the code is in the same source file as the declaration or in a different file. This is because functions are global by default. After the different source files have been compiled to object code, a tool called the *linker* then performs the task of resolving undefined symbols in each object file. When it finds a call to an undefined function in one object file, it searches the other object files that comprise the application together with any libraries specified until it finds it. If no match is found, the linker will fail with an undefined symbol error.

When calling a function from a separate source file, however, it is important to be aware of the need to declare a function prototype to avoid compilation warnings.

20.5 **Function Prototypes**

Where a function is declared in relation to where it is called from can be a significant factor. In the same way that many cultures read a page from top to bottom, a compiler also reads an Objective-C source file from top to bottom. If the compiler comes across a call to a function before it has found the function declaration it has to make assumptions about the type of result that function returns. The default assumption is that the function will return an *int*. Having made this assumption, if when the compiler finally reaches the function declaration, an error will have to be reported if it is found to return a data type other than an *int*. To see this in action, try compiling the following code:

```
#import <Foundation/Foundation.h>

int main (int argc, const char * argv[])
{
    @autoreleasepool {
        float result;

        result = multiply( 10, 20 );
    }
    return 0;
}

float multiply (int x, int y)
{
        return x * y;
}
```

When an attempt to compile the above code is made, the compilation will fail with the following message:

```
warning: implicit declaration of function 'multiply' is invalid in
    C99 [-Wimplicit-function-declaration]
error: conflicting types for 'multiply'
main.m:8:18:note: previous implicit declaration is here
```

The compiler is complaining because it had assumed when the function was called at line 8 that it returned an *int* because up until that point it had not found a function declaration to tell it otherwise. Having made this assumption it then found the function declaration and discovered it actually returned a *float*, thereby causing a conflict.

There are two solutions to this problem. One is to always declare functions before they are called:

```
#import <Foundation/Foundation.h>

float multiply (int x, int y)
{
        return x * y;
}

int main (int argc, const char * argv[])
{
    @autoreleasepool {
        float result;

        result = multiply( 10, 20 );
    }
    return 0;
}
```

This is a work around for simple cases but can quickly become unmanageable in larger application code bases with multiple files and functions calling other functions. A much better solution is to use a *function prototype*. This is a declaration that can be placed at the top of code files that pre-declares the return type and arguments of a function. For example, the function prototype for our *multiply* function is as follows:

```
float multiply (int x, int y);
```

The argument names in the function prototype are entirely optional and the same result can be achieved with just the argument types:

```
float multiply (int, int);
```

An Overview of Objective-C Functions

Note that the semi-colon (;) is mandatory.

We can now apply this concept to our earlier example:

```
#import <Foundation/Foundation.h>

float multiply (int, int);

int main (int argc, const char * argv[])
{
    @autoreleasepool {
        float result;

        result = multiply( 10, 20 );
    }
    return 0;
}

float multiply (int x, int y)
{
        return x * y;
}
```

For functions that accept a variable number of arguments, the '...' directive can be used in the function prototype:

```
int addAll (int, ...);
```

The steps are similar when making a call from one source code file to a function that resides in a separate source file. When the compiler is unable to find the implementation of the function in the file from which it is called, a warning will be reported. Keep in mind that this is just a warning and that the function will be found during the link phase and the program will run without error.

To avoid such compilation warnings, simply place a function prototype at the top of the source from which the function call is being made, pre-fixing the declaration with the *extern* keyword to notify the compiler that the function implementation resides in an external file.

```
extern float multiply (int, int);
```

20.6 **Function Scope and the static Specifier**

Objective-C functions are considered by default to be global in scope. This means that a function declared in one file in a program can be called from any other code file in the program. This means that function names must be unique. Two functions with the same name will cause an error when the code is linked during the build process. To confine the scope of a function to the file in which it is declared, simply prefix the declaration with the *static* keyword:

```
static float multiply (int x, int y)
{
        return x * y;
}
```

20.7 **Static Variables in Functions**

In the normal course of program execution, any variables declared locally in a function are discarded when the function exits and execution returns to the code location from where the call was made. For example, each time the *displayit* function is called in the following code, variable *y* is re-initialized to 0:

```
#import <Foundation/Foundation.h>

void displayit (int);

int main (int argc, const char * argv[])
{
    @autoreleasepool {
        int i;

        for (i=0; i<5; i++)
        {
                displayit( i );
        }
    }
```

```
    return 0;
}


void displayit (int i)
{
    int y = 0;
    y += i;
    NSLog (@"y + i = %i", y);
}
```

When executed we get the following output from the above code:

```
2009-10-20 15:39:12.306 t[10128:10b] y + i = 0
2009-10-20 15:39:12.308 t[10128:10b] y + i = 1
2009-10-20 15:39:12.308 t[10128:10b] y + i = 2
2009-10-20 15:39:12.309 t[10128:10b] y + i = 3
2009-10-20 15:39:12.309 t[10128:10b] y + i = 4
```

If we want the value of y to be retained after the function has executed, we simply declare the variable as *static*:

```
static int y = 0;
```

Now, when the code is compiled and run, we get the following output because the value of y is not being reset to 0 each time the function is called:

```
2009-10-20 15:39:32.194 t[10136:10b] y + i = 0
2009-10-20 15:39:32.195 t[10136:10b] y + i = 1
2009-10-20 15:39:32.195 t[10136:10b] y + i = 3
2009-10-20 15:39:32.196 t[10136:10b] y + i = 6
2009-10-20 15:39:32.196 t[10136:10b] y + i = 10
```

20.8 Summary

A function is a named block of code that can be called upon to perform a specific task and provides a mechanism for structuring code and promoting reuse. Functions can be provided data on which to perform a task in the form of arguments and can be designed to return a result. This chapter has introduced the concepts of functions and explored the necessity to use function prototypes, particularly when calling a function that resides in a different source file.

21. Objective-C Enumerators

Objective-C Enumerators allow variables to be declared with a predefined list of valid values, each of which is assigned a name that can be used when setting the variable. This has the advantage of making the code easier to read and understand.

21.1 Why Use Enumerators

As previously described, enumerators allow the programmer to predefine the range of values that can be assigned to a variable and use self-explanatory names when setting those values. The benefits of this are twofold. Firstly this makes code easier to read and understand. Secondly this, to a certain extent, allows control of the values that can be assigned (though as we will see later in this chapter, enforcement is rather weak).

21.2 Declaring an Enumeration

The syntax for declaring an enumeration is as follows:

```
enum <name> { <value name 1>, <value name 2>, ... };
```

In the above syntax outline, *enum* is the keyword that tells the compiler we are creating an enumeration, *<name>* is the name to be assigned to the enumeration and the *<value name>* fields are the names that can be used to set the variable. Internally, enumerators use numbers corresponding to the value names. By default the first value corresponds to 0, the second to 1 and so on. It is also possible to specify the values used by each value name:

```
enum <name> { <value name 1> = <value1>, <value name 2> = <value2>,
... };
```

For example, we can specify an enumeration for the days of the week:

```
enum daysofweek {monday, tuesday, wednesday, thursday, friday,
saturday, sunday};
```

In the above construct, monday is equal to 0, tuesday is 1 and so on. If we specify a number for just one entry, the remaining values will follow on from that number. For example:

```
enum daysofweek {monday = 1, tuesday, wednesday, thursday, friday,
saturday, sunday};
```

In this case, monday will be 1, tuesday will be 2 and so on.

Alternatively we can specify a value for each entry in the enumeration:

```
enum temperature {cold = 5, warm = 50, hot = 95};
```

21.3 **Creating and Using an Enumeration**

Having declared an enumeration, the next step is to declare a variable of that type. For example, to create a variable called *currentTemp* from our *temperature* enumerator type we would write the following code:

```
enum temperature currentTemp;
```

Now that we have created a variable based on our enumerator data type, we can try setting a value using one of the value names and then displaying the current value of the variable:

```
currentTemp = hot;
NSLog (@"Current temperature is %i", currentTemp);
```

When compiled and executed, the above code will output the following:

```
Current temperature is 95
```

As we can see, although we assigned *hot* to our *currentTemp* variable, Objective-C translated it to the corresponding number 95. If we attempt to assign a value using an undefined name as follows, the code will fail to compile with a *'tepid'* *undeclared* error message:

```
currentTemp = tepid;
```

We can, however, bypass this system by assigning a number directly to the variable:

```
currentTemp = 109;
```

The above code will, unfortunately, compile and run.

21.4 **Enumerators and Variable Names**

When using enumerators in Objective-C, it is important to be aware that both the enumerator name and the value names are treated as symbols that must be unique within the given scope. For example, because we use the value name *hot* in our *temperature* enumerator we cannot then use *hot* as a variable name within the same scope (for information on variable scope refer to *Objective-C Variable Scope and Storage Class*). Take, for the example, the following code. Here we have our temperature enumerator and also a declaration for a variable named *hot*:

```
enum temperature {cold = 5, warm = 50, hot = 95};

enum temperature currentTemp;

int hot = 100;

currentTemp = hot;

NSLog (@"Current temperature is %i", currentTemp);
```

If we attempt to compile this code, an error will result informing us that a duplicate symbol has been detected:

```
temp.m: In function 'main':
temp.m:14: error: 'hot' redeclared as different kind of symbol
temp.m:10: error: previous definition of 'hot' was here
```

21.5 **Summary**

This chapter has covered the topic of enumerators in Objective-C. Enumerators allow the programmer to predefine the range of values that can be assigned to a variable and use self-explanatory names when subsequently setting those values in the application code.

22. An Overview of the Objective-C Foundation Framework

In previous chapters of *Objective-C 2.0 Essentials* we have covered the concept of object-oriented programming in considerable detail. So far, however, we have focused almost exclusively on how to create and work with our own classes and objects within Objective-C programs.

Now that we have a firm understanding of how to work with objects we can apply what we have learned to using a set of pre-existing classes that are provided with Objective-C to make our jobs as programmers much easier. These classes belong to the *Foundation Framework*.

22.1 The Foundation Framework

The Objective-C Foundation Framework is essentially a set of classes that are provided to speed and ease the process of developing applications using Objective-C. The framework was developed by NeXT Computer as part of the NeXTStep environment. When NeXT was acquired by Apple, Inc. the Foundation classes quickly became of basis of Mac OS X and then the iOS development kit. For a full history of how this came to be, refer to *The History of Objective-C*.

Due to the fact that the Foundation Framework started life of part of NeXTstep, the classes that comprise this framework all begin with the letters "NS".

You will recall that when we created our first class in *An Overview of Objective-C Object Oriented Programming* we derived our class from *NSObject*. NSObject is a part of the Foundation Framework and as you become more familiar with the framework you will learn that most Foundation classes are derived from this class. In this and subsequent chapters we will look in more detail at some of the other classes provided by the framework.

22.2 **Including the Foundation Headers**

In previous chapters we have been including the header files for the Foundation Framework in our examples. This is achieved using the following line of code:

```
#import <Foundation/Foundation.h>
```

In fact, if we don't want to have to worry about including the header file for each Foundation class we wish to use in a code file, this is all we need to do. Alternatively, we can selectively include the header files for only the classes we intend to use. For example, the following code imports only the headers we need:

```
#import <Foundation/NSObject.h>
#import <Foundation/NSString.h>
#import <Foundation/NSAutoreleasePool.h>

int main (int argc, const char * argv[])
{
    @autoreleasepool {
        NSString *myString = @"Hello";
    }
    return 0;
}
```

22.3 **Finding the Foundation Framework Documentation**

A detailed overview of every class and method in the Foundation Framework is beyond the scope of this book and would be largely redundant given that this information is already provided by Apple in various locations. Instead, this book will focus on teaching you how to use the most common Foundation classes to work with numbers, strings, arrays, dictionaries and file systems. This knowledge, combined with the Apple Foundation documentation should be all you need to begin working proficiently with these classes.

The Foundation documentation may be accessed via the Apple web site at:

http://developer.apple.com/mac/library/documentation/Cocoa/Reference/Foundation/ObjC_classic /

The Framework Reference Documentation lists all the classes available and for each class describes in detail what the class does and what methods are available. In the following chapters we will look in detail at how to work with some of these classes.

23. Working with String Objects in Objective-C

Strings are collections of characters that are grouped together to form words or sentences. If it wasn't for humans, computers would probably never have anything to do with strings. The fact is, however, that one of the primary jobs of a computer is to accept data from and present data to humans. For this reason it is highly likely that any Objective-C program is going to involve a considerable amount of code specifically designed to work with data in the form of strings. The purpose of this chapter is to cover the key aspects of string creation, comparison and manipulation in Objective-C using the Foundation Framework's NSString class.

23.1 Strings without NSString

As we've already discussed, Objective-C is built upon the C programming language. C also has a mechanism for dealing with strings, but because C is not an object oriented programming language it does not have any of the advantages offered to us through the NSString class. For example, to use the C approach to creating strings we have to set up a pointer to a string of characters:

```
char *myString = "This is a C character string";
```

Alternatively, we could define a C style character array to contain a string:

```
char myString[] = "This is a C character array";
```

Having created the string we literally have nothing but a section of memory where a null terminated string of characters is located. If we want to do anything to manipulate the string we will have to write our own code to do it.

By using NSString, however, we get access to a wide range of methods provided with that class to manipulate our string without having to write all the code ourselves. My first ever job involved writing complex programs in the C programming language, and from bitter experience I can tell you that the hardest part of that job was writing code to work with strings. My life would have been much easier if Objective-C and the NSString class had existed all those years ago.

In addition, C style character strings are composed of single byte characters and therefore limited in the range of characters that can be stored. This usually becomes a problem when dealing with non-ASCII character sets used by foreign languages. NSString objects, on the other hand, are comprised of multibyte Unicode characters and can handle just about any language character set.

23.2 **Declaring Constant String Objects**

A constant string object is declared by encapsulating the string in double quotes (") preceded by an @ sign. For example:

```
@"This is a constant character string object";
```

In order to display the current value of a string object using NSLog, simply reference the string using '%@' as follows:

```
NSLog (@"%@", @"This is a constant character string object");
```

Even though all we are doing here is creating a constant string object, keep in mind that this is still an object. As such, it has a range of methods that we can call on it. For example string objects have a *length* method that returns the number of characters in the string. We can, therefore, call this on a constant string object:

```
int len = [@"Hello" length];

NSLog (@"Length of string = %i", len);
```

The above code declares a constant string object containing the word "Hello" and calls the *length* method of the object. The result is assigned to an integer variable named *len* which in turn is displayed using NSLog. When compiled and executed, we get the following output:

```
Length of string = 5
```

Constant string objects are actually instantiated from the NSConstantString class which, much like the other classes we will look at in this chapter, is actually a subclass of the NSString class. In practice, given the way that constant strings are used, it is unlikely that you will need to specifically declare your string constants as being of type NSConstantString. It is more likely that you will declare the string as we have done in this section and let the compiler handle the rest.

23.3 Creating Mutable and Immutable String Objects

Two additional types of Objective-C string objects are *mutable* and *immutable*. When you create a string object of type *NSString* you are creating an *immutable* string object. This means that once a string has been assigned to the object, that string cannot subsequently be modified in any way.

```
NSString *string1 = @"This string is immutable";
```

Mutable string objects, on the other hand, are declared using the *NSMutableString* class and allow the string contained within the object to be modified using a variety of methods (some of which will be covered in the remainder of this chapter). NSMutableString is a subclass of NSString, which in turn is a subclass of NSObject. Mutable strings cannot be initialized simply by assigning a constant string object as we did above since that will just give us a pointer to an immutable constant string object. Instead, the string constant must be copied into the mutable string object. For example:

```
NSMutableString *string2 = [NSMutableString stringWithString: @"This
string is mutable"];
```

Once a string has been declared as immutable, the only way to get a mutable version of the string is to create a mutable string object and copy the contents of the immutable string object to it. This can be achieved using the NSMutableString *stringWithString* class method. For example:

```
NSString *string1 = @"This is a string";
NSMutableString *string2;

string2 = [NSMutableString stringWithString: string1];
```

Once executed, the above code will create an immutable string object (string1) initialized with the text "This is a string" and an empty pointer to an immutable string object (string2). The *stringWithString* class method of the NSMutableString class is then called, passing through the immutable string1 as an argument. This method returns a new object containing the immutable string and assigns it to string2. We now have a mutable copy of the immutable string1 object.

23.4 **Getting the Length of a String**

The length of the string in a string object can be obtained by accessing the *length* method of the string object:

```
NSString *string1 = @"This string is Immutable";

int len = [string1 length];

NSLog (@"String length is %i", len);
```

The above code fragment will produce the following output when executed:

```
String length is 24
```

Alternatively, the *length* property of a string object may be accessed using dot notation:

```
int len = string1.length;
```

23.5 **Copying a String**

When copying one string object to another it might be tempting to think that you can simply assign the object from one variable to another. For example, if we had two integer variables and wanted to assign the value of one to the other we could simply do the following:

```
int a = 10;
int b;

b = a;
```

After the above code has executed, both variables *a* and *b* will contain the value *10*. The same is not, however, true of string objects. Take for example the following code fragment:

```
NSMutableString *string1;
NSMutableString *string2;

string1 = [NSMutableString stringWithString: @"This is a string"];

string2 = string1;
```

What we have achieved here is to create two variables (string1 and string2) that *point* to the memory location of the same string object. This is because the '*' before the variable names in the declarations indicate that these are pointers to objects, not actual objects. Any time that we access the object referenced by either of these pointers we will, in fact, be accessing the same object. To prove this, we can make a change using the string2 reference and then display the string associated with both the string1 and string2 object pointers:

```
NSMutableString *string1;
NSMutableString *string2;

string1 = [NSMutableString stringWithString: @"This is a string"];

string2 = string1;

[string2 appendString: @" and it is mine!"];

NSLog (@"string1 = %@", string1);

NSLog (@"string2 = %@", string2);
```

The above code will display the following output, proving that both string1 and string2 point to the same object since only one reference was modified, yet both show the change:

```
string1 = This is a string and it is mine!
string2 = This is a string and it is mine!
```

To actually copy one string object to another string object we must use the stringWithString method of the NSMutableString class:

```
NSMutableString *string1;
NSMutableString *string2;


string1 = [NSMutableString stringWithString: @"This is a string"]; //
Initialize string1

string2 = [NSMutableString stringWithString: string1]; // Copy
string1 object to string2

[string2 appendString: @" and it is mine!"]; // Modify string2

NSLog (@"string1 = %@", string1);

NSLog (@"string2 = %@", string2);
```

When executed, the appended text appears only in the object referenced by string2 since string2 now references a different object to that referenced by string1:

```
2009-11-03 14:42:10.426 t[32263:10b] string1 = This is a string
2009-11-03 14:42:10.427 t[32263:10b] string2 = This is a string and
it is mine!
```

It is also possible to create a mutable copy of an NSString object by calling the object's *mutableCopy* method as follows:

```
NSMutableString *string1;
NSMutableString *string2;


string1 = [NSMutableString stringWithString: @"This is a string"]; //
Initialize string1

string2 = [string1 mutableCopy]; // Copy string1 object to string2
```

23.6 **Searching for a Substring**

A common requirement when working with strings is to identify whether a particular sequence of characters appears within a string. This can be achieved using the *rangeOfString* method. This method returns a structure of type *NSRange*. The NSRange structure contains a *location* value providing the index into the string of the matched substring and a length value indicating the length of the match.

```
NSString *string1 = @"The quick brown fox jumped";


NSRange match = [string1 rangeOfString: @"brown fox"];
NSLog (@"match found at index %lu", match.location);
NSLog (@"match length = %lu", match.length);
```

The NSLog call will display the location and length of the match. Note that the location is an index into the string where the match started and that the index considers the first position in a string to be 0 and not 1. As such, the location in our example will be 10 and the length will be 9.

In the event that no match is found, the *rangeOfString* method will set the location member of the NSRange structure to *NSNotFound*. For example:

```
NSString *string1 = @"The quick brown fox jumped";

NSRange match = [string1 rangeOfString: @"brown dog"];

if (match.location == NSNotFound)
        NSLog (@"Match not found");
else
        NSLog (@"match found at index %lu", match.location);
```

23.7 **Replacing Parts of a String**

Sections of a mutable string may be replaced by other character sequences using the *replaceCharactersInRange* method. This method directly modifies the string object on which the method is called so only works on mutable string objects.

This method requires two arguments. The first argument is an NSRange structure consisting of the location of the first character and the total number of characters to be replaced. The second argument is the replacement string. An NSRange structure can be created by calling *NSMakeRange* and passing through the location and length values as arguments. For example, to replace the word "fox" with "squirrel" in our sample mutable string object we would write the following Objective-C code:

```
NSMutableString *string1 = [NSMutableString stringWithString: @"The
quick brown fox jumped"];


[string1 replaceCharactersInRange: NSMakeRange(16, 3) withString:
@"squirrel"];


NSLog (@"string1 = %@", string1);
```

As you may have noted from the above example, the replacement string does not have to be the same length as the range being replaced. The string object and replacement method will resize the string automatically.

23.8 **String Search and Replace**

Previously we have covered how to perform a search in a string and how to replace a subsection of a string using the *rangeOfString* and *replaceCharactersInRange* methods respectively. The fact that both of these methods use the NSRange structure enables us to combine the two methods to perform a search and replace. In the following example, we use *rangeOfString* to provide us with an NSRange structure for the substring to be replaced and then pass this through to *replaceCharactersInRange* to perform the replacement:

```
NSMutableString *string1 = [NSMutableString stringWithString: @"The
quick brown fox jumped"];


[string1 replaceCharactersInRange: [string1 rangeOfString: @"brown
fox"] withString: @"black dog"];
```

When executed, *string1* will contain the string "The quick black dog jumped".

23.9 Deleting Sections of a String

Similar techniques to those described above can be used to delete a subsection of a string using the *deleteCharactersInRange* method. As with the preceding examples, this method accepts an NSRange structure as an argument and can be combined with the *rangeOfString* method to perform a search and delete:

```
NSMutableString *string1 = [NSMutableString stringWithString: @"The
quick brown fox jumped"];

[string1 deleteCharactersInRange: [string1 rangeOfString:
@"jumped"]];
```

23.10 Extracting a Subsection of a String

A subsection of a string can be extracted using the *substringWithRange* method. The range is specified using an *NSRange* structure and the extracted substring is returned in the form of an NSString object:

```
NSMutableString *string1 = [NSMutableString stringWithString: @"The
quick brown fox jumped"];
NSString *string2;

string2 = [string1 substringWithRange: NSMakeRange (4, 5)];

NSLog (@"string2 = %@", string2);
```

When executed, the above code will output the substring assigned to *string2* ("quick").

Alternatively, a substring may be extracted from a given index until the end of the string using the *subStringFromIndex* method. For example:

```
NSMutableString *string1 = [NSMutableString stringWithString: @"The
quick brown fox jumped"];
NSString *string2;

string2 = [string1 substringFromIndex: 4];
```

Similarly, *subStringToIndex* may be used to extract a substring from the beginning of the source string up until a specified character index into the string.

23.11 **Inserting Text into a String**

The *insertString* method inserts a substring into a string object and takes as arguments the NSString object from which the new string is to be inserted and the index location into the target string where the insertion is to be performed:

```
NSMutableString *string1 = [NSMutableString stringWithString: @"The
quick brown fox jumped"];

[string1 insertString: @"agile, " atIndex: 4];
```

23.12 **Appending Text to the End of a String**

Text can be appended to the end of an existing string object using the *appendString* method. This method directly modifies the string object on which the method is called and as such is only available for mutable string objects.

```
NSMutableString *string1 = [NSMutableString stringWithString: @"The
quick brown fox jumped"];

[string1 appendString: @" over the lazy dog"];

NSLog (@"string1 = %@", string1);
```

23.13 **Comparing Strings**

To compare the strings contained within two string objects we can use the *isEqualToString* method:

```
NSString *string1 = @"My String";
NSString *string2 = @"My String 2";

if ([string1 isEqualToString: string2])
        NSLog (@"Strings match");
else
```

```
NSLog (@"Strings do not match");
```

Another option is to use the *compare* method (to perform a case sensitive comparison) or the *caseInsenstiveCompare* NSString methods. These are more advanced comparison methods that can be useful when sorting strings into order.

23.14 **Checking for String Prefixes and Suffixes**

A string object can be tested to identify whether the string begins or ends with a particular sequence of characters (otherwise known as prefixes and suffixes). This is achieved using the *hasPrefix* and *hasSuffix* methods respectively, both of which return boolean values based on whether a match is found or not.

```
NSString *string1 = @"The quick brown fox jumped";

BOOL result;

result = [string1 hasPrefix: @"The"];

if (result)
        NSLog (@"String begins with The");

result = [string1 hasSuffix: @"dog"];

if (result)
        NSLog (@"String ends with dog");
```

23.15 **Converting to Upper or Lower Case**

The Foundation NSString classes provide a variety of methods for modifying different aspects of case within a string. Note that each of these methods returns a new string object reflecting the change, leaving the original string object unchanged.

- **capitalizedString**

Returns a copy of the specified string with the first letter of each word capitalized and all other characters in lower case:

```
NSString *string1 = @"The quicK brOwn fox jumpeD";
NSString *string2;

string2 = [string1 capitalizedString];
```

The above code will return a string object containing the string "The Quick Brown Fox Jumped" and assign it to the string2 variable. The string object referenced by string1 remains unmodified.

- **lowercaseString**

Returns a copy of the specified string with all characters in lower case:

```
NSString *string1 = @"The quicK brOwn fox jumpeD";
NSString *string2;

string2 = [string1 lowercaseString];
```

The above code will return a string object containing the string "the quick brown fox jumped" and assign it to the string2 variable. The string object referenced by string1 remains unmodified.

- **uppercaseString**

Returns a copy of the specified string with all characters in upper case:

```
NSString *string1 = @"The quicK brOwn fox jumpeD";
NSString *string2;

string2 = [string1 uppercaseString];
```

The above code will return a string object containing the string "THE QUICK BROWN FOX JUMPED" and assign it to the string2 variable. The string object referenced by string1 remains unmodified.

23.16 Converting Strings to Numbers

String objects can be converted to a variety of number types:

- **Convert String to int**

```
NSString *string1 = @"10";
int myInt = [string1 intValue];
NSLog (@"%i", myInt);
```

- **Convert String to double**

```
NSString *string1 = @"10.1092";
double myDouble = [string1 doubleValue];
NSLog (@"%f", myDouble);
```

- **Convert String to float**

```
NSString *string1 = @"10.1092";
float myFloat = [string1 floatValue];
NSLog (@"%f", myFloat);
```

- **Convert String to NSInteger**

```
NSString *string1 = @"10";
NSInteger myInteger = [string1 integerValue];
NSLog (@"%li", myInteger);
```

23.17 Converting a String Object to ASCII

The string contained within a string object can be extracted and converted to an ASCII C style character string using the *UTF8String* method. For example:

```
NSString *string1 = @"The quick brown fox";
const char *utfString = [string1 UTF8String];
printf ("Converted string = %s\n", utfString);
```

23.18 Summary

One of the most flexible and widely used classes of the Objective-C Foundation Framework is the NSString class. This class consists of a wide range of methods that can be used to manipulate string based data, including search and replace, copying and number to string conversion.

24. Understanding Objective-C Number Objects

In the chapter entitled *Objective-C 2.0 Data Types* we looked at the basic data types supported by Objective-C including a range of types for working with numbers. These data types are what are known as *primitive types* in that they simply allow values to be stored in memory and are not objects.

In order to work with numbers in object form, Objective-C provides the *NSNumber* class. This class is one of the stranger additions to the Objective-C language in that functionally speaking, number objects don't give you anything that you can't already do with primitive number types. It seems the sole purpose of the NSNumber class is to allow numbers to be stored in an NSArray object, which only handles objects. Numbers that are wrapped in an object are referred to as *boxed values*.

In this chapter we will take a look at the NSNumber class and provide an overview of how to work with number objects.

24.1 Creating and Initializing NSNumber Objects

As previously discussed, the primary purpose of the NSNumber class is to allow the storage of primitive numerical data in the form of an object. The NSNumber class is able to store signed and unsigned char, short, integer, int, long and long long data types and also float, double and Bool values.

The NSNumber class contains a set of class methods designed specifically for creating objects and initializing them with values of a particular numerical data type. The naming convention for these class methods is as follows:

```
numberWith<Unsigned><Type>
```

The full list of creation and initialization methods is as follows:

```
numberWithBool
numberWithChar
numberWithDouble
numberWithFloat
numberWithInt
numberWithInteger
numberWithLong
numberWithLongLong
numberWithShort
numberWithUnsignedChar
numberWithUnsignedInt
numberWithUnsignedInteger
numberWithUnsignedLong
numberWithUnsignedLongLong
numberWithUnsignedShort
```

Because these are class methods, rather than instance methods, they are called on the class rather than on an existing object. For example, to create an NSNumber object called myFloat, configured to hold a float value, we could write the following code:

```
NSNumber *myFloat;
myFloat = [NSNumber numberWithFloat: 10.09];
```

Once executed, the above code will create a new NSNumber object and assign the floating point value of 10.09 to it.

24.2 Initialization using NSNumber Literals

NSNumber objects may also be initialized using the recently introduced Modern Objective-C number literals syntax. This allows an NSNumber object to be initialized using the assignment operator followed by the value to be assigned prefixed with an '@' character and followed by a suffix indicating the type. Consider, for example, the following method based syntax to assign an integer to an NSNumber object:

```
NSNumber *number = [NSNumber numberWithInt:256];
```

Using NSNumber literals, the same result may be achieved using the following syntax:

```
NSNumber *myInteger = @256;
```

Clearly this Modern Objective-C syntax saves a considerable amount of typing on the part of the programmer and also serves to make the code easier to read. Note that in the absence of a suffix, as in the above example, Objective-C assumes by default that the number being assigned to the NSNumber object is an integer type. If a decimal place is included in the assigned value, on the other hand, the compiler assumes that the value is of double type. The following code fragment, therefore, is equivalent to using the *numberWithDouble:* method:

```
NSNumber *myDouble = @4.5689432;
```

Similarly, a character wrapped in single quotation characters is assumed to be of type char. Consider, for example, the method based approach to creating an NSNumber object with a character:

```
NSNumber *myChar = [NSNumber numberWithChar:'Z'];
```

Using **NSNumber** literals, this can more easily be expressed as follows:

```
NSNumber *myChar = @'Z';
```

NSNumber objects may be initialized with Boolean values simply by assigning YES or NO, once again prefixed with the '@' character:

```
NSNumber *myBool = @YES;
```

Finally, other number types may be specified through the use of suffixes. For example:

```
NSNumber *number;

number = @256u; // Unsigned Int
number = @54761 // Long
number = @43231ul // Unsigned Long
number = @1234311l // Long Long
number = @1254.23f // Float
```

24.3 **Getting the Value of a Number Object**

The current value stored in a number object can be obtained using one of a number of retrieval instance methods. The type of value retrieved depends on the method used. The full list of retrieval instance methods is as follows:

```
boolValue
charValue
decimalValue
doubleValue
floatValue
intValue
integerValue
longLongValue
longValue
shortValue
unsignedCharValue
unsignedIntegerValue
unsignedIntValue
unsignedLongLongValue
unsignedLongValue
unsignedShortValue
```

For example, we can extend our example to retrieve and display the value stored in our number object as follows:

```
NSNumber *myFloat;
float floatvalue;


myFloat = [NSNumber numberWithDouble: 10.09];


floatvalue = [myFloat floatValue];


NSLog (@"Value = %f", floatvalue);
```

Note that the method used to retrieve the value stored in a number object must match the method used to store the object. An attempt, for example, to retrieve a char from an object initialized as a double will provide an unexpected result.

24.4 **Comparing Number Objects**

To compare the values stored in two number objects it is necessary to use either the *isEqualToNumber* or *compare* methods. These are both instance methods, and as such are called on one object instance, passing through the second object as an argument.

The *isEqualToNumber* method returns a Boolean value depending on whether the two objects contain the same numbers. For example:

```
NSNumber *myFloat1;
NSNumber *myFloat2;

myFloat1 = [NSNumber numberWithDouble: 10.09];
myFloat2 = [NSNumber numberWithDouble: 10.08];

if ([myFloat1 isEqualToNumber: myFloat2])
        NSLog (@"Numbers are equal");
else
        NSLog (@"Numbers are not equal");
```

The *compare* method is used when you need to know whether one number is less than, greater than or equal to another when those numbers are held in number objects. The method returns the result of the comparison in the form of an NSComparisonResult enumeration. Possible settings are *NSOrderedSame* if the numbers are equal, *NSOrderedAscending* if the value stored in the first object is less than the number stored in the second and *NSOrderedDescending* if the opposite is true:

```
NSNumber *myFloat1;
NSNumber *myFloat2;

myFloat1 = [NSNumber numberWithDouble: 10.09];
myFloat2 = [NSNumber numberWithDouble: 10.08];
NSComparisonResult result;

result = [myFloat1 compare: myFloat2];

if (result == NSOrderedSame)
```

```
        NSLog(@"Numbers are equal");
else if (result == NSOrderedAscending)
        NSLog(@"Float1 is less than Float2");
else if (result == NSOrderedDescending)
        NSLog(@"Float1 is greater than Float2");
```

24.5 **Getting the Number Object Value as a String**

In order to convert the value stored in a number object to a string, the *stringValue* instance method is provided by the NSNumber class. This method returns the current value as a string object (for more information on string objects refer to *Working with String Objects in Objective-C*):

```
NSNumber *myFloat;

NSString *myString;

myFloat = [NSNumber numberWithDouble: 10.09];

myString = [myFloat stringValue];

NSLog (@"Number as string is %@", myString);
```

24.6 **Summary**

The NSNumber class provides an alternative to using primitive types and a way to store numbers in objects. This is of particular significance when numbers need to be stored in an NSArray or NSDictionary object since these classes are not able to store primitive types. NSNumber object instances may be initialized using either class methods or NSNumber literal syntax.

25. Working with Objective-C Array Objects

An array is an object that contains collections of other objects. Array objects in Objective-C are handled using the Foundation Framework *NSArray* class. The NSArray class contains a number of methods specifically designed to ease the creation and manipulation of arrays within Objective-C programs. Unlike some object oriented programming languages (C# being one example), the objects contained in an array do not all have to be of the same type.

In this chapter, we will cover some of the basics of working with array objects in Objective-C. Many more class and instance methods are provided by the array classes than can be covered here so refer to the Foundation Framework documentation for a full listing of capabilities.

25.1 Mutable and Immutable Arrays

Array objects in Objective-C come in mutable and immutable forms. The contents of immutable arrays cannot be changed after the array has been initialized. Immutable arrays are instantiated from the NSArray class. Mutable arrays are created using the NSMutableArray class (a subclass of NSArray) and can be modified after they have been created and initialized.

25.2 Creating an Array Object using Class Methods

NSArray objects may be initialized either using class methods, or the Modern Objective-C Array literals syntax. The NSArray class contains a class method named *arrayWithObjects* that can be called upon to create a new array object and initialize it with elements. For example:

```
NSArray *myColors;
```

```
myColors = [NSArray arrayWithObjects: @"Red", @"Green", @"Blue",
@"Yellow", nil];
```

The above code creates a new array object called *myColors* and initializes it with four constant string objects containing the strings "Red", "Green", "Blue" and "Yellow". A *nil* entry is required so that the methods called upon to work on the array know where the end of the array is located. Failure to include this entry may result in the application crashing, particularly during sort operations.

Because we used the NSArray class in the above example, the contents of the array object cannot be changed subsequent to initialization. To create a mutable array that will allow the array contents to be modified, we need to use the NSMutableArray class:

```
NSMutableArray *myColors;

myColors = [NSMutableArray arrayWithObjects: @"Red", @"Green",
@"Blue", @"Yellow", nil];
```

25.3 Creating an Array Object using Literal Syntax

As was the case with NSNumber objects, Modern Objective-C provides a more programmer friendly approach to Array initialization through the implementation of Array literal syntax. This involves use of the assignment operator followed by the list of array elements prefixed with the '@' character then wrapped in square brackets. The previous initialization code can instead be represented as follows:

```
NSArray *myColors;

myColors = @[@"Red", @"Green", @"Blue", @"Yellow"];
```

Note that with the use of literal syntax it is no longer necessary to terminate the array with a *nil* value.

It is important to keep in mind that array literal syntax creates immutable arrays by default. If a mutable array is required when using this syntax, the *mutableCopy* method of the object must be called. For example:

```
NSMutableArray *myColors = [@[@"Red", @"Green", @"Blue", @"Yellow"]
mutableCopy];
```

25.4 Finding out the Number of Elements in an Array

The number of objects in an array (referred to as *elements*) can be identified using the *count* instance method of the NSArray class:

```
NSArray *myColors;

myColors = @[@"Red", @"Green", @"Blue", @"Yellow"];

NSLog (@"Number of elements in array = %lu", [myColors count]);
```

When executed, the above code will output the following:

```
Number of elements in array = 4
```

The same result may also be achieved using dot notation to access the *count* property of the NSArray object:

```
myColors.count;
```

25.5 Accessing the Elements of an Array Object using Methods

The objects contained in an array are given index positions beginning at position zero. Each element may be accessed by passing the required index position through as an argument to the NSArray *objectAtIndex* instance method. We can, therefore, now extend our array example to display each element, using the count method to identify in advance how many elements there are to display:

```
NSArray *myColors;
int i;
int count;

myColors = @[@"Red", @"Green", @"Blue", @"Yellow"];
count = myColors.count;
```

```
for (i = 0; i < count; i++)
        NSLog (@"Element %i = %@", i, [myColors objectAtIndex: i]);
```

When run, the above code will display each element in the array object:

```
Element 0 = Red
Element 1 = Green
Element 2 = Blue
Element 3 = Yellow
```

25.6 Accessing Array Elements using Index Subscripting

Indexing subscripting is a feature which is present in most other programming languages (Java, C, C# and C++ being notable examples) but has only recently been added to Objective-C. In actual fact, Objective-C could easily have adopted index subscripting as part of its C Programming Language origins but did not.

Index subscripting allows the element in an array to be referenced by suffixing the array name with the index value of the required element wrapped in square brackets. The following code, for example, uses the *objectAtIndex:* method to access the element at index position 1 of our myColors array:

```
NSString *secondColor = [myColors objectAtIndex: 1];
```

Using index subscripting, however, the same result may more easily be achieved as follows:

```
NSString *secondColor = myColors[1];
```

Index subscripting may also be used to replace one object at an index with another. The following code, for example, replaces the string "Yellow" at index position 3 with "Orange" (note the creation of a mutable array to allow the element to be modified):

```
NSMutableArray *myColors = [@[@"Red", @"Green", @"Blue", @"Yellow"]
mutableCopy];
myColors[3] = @"Orange";
```

25.7 **Accessing Array Elements using Fast Enumeration**

The technique for accessing all the array elements using a *for* loop as described in a previous section is a little ungainly. Another, easier mechanism for accessing elements in an array involves something called *fast enumeration*. Fast enumeration simply requires that a variable be declared to hold each array element, and then referenced in the *for* loop:

```
NSArray *myColors;
NSString *color;


myColors = @[@"Red", @"Green", @"Blue", @"Yellow"];


for (color in myColors)
        NSLog (@"Element = %@", color);
```

25.8 **Adding Elements to an Array Object**

New elements may be added to a mutable array object using the *addObject* instance method of the NSMutableArray class. For example, to declare and initialize an array, and then later add new element objects the following code might be used:

```
NSMutableArray *myColors;


myColors = @[@"Red", @"Green", @"Blue", @"Yellow"];


[myColors addObject: @"Indigo"];
[myColors addObject: @"Violet"];
```

25.9 **Inserting Elements into an Array**

The previous method appends new objects onto the end of an array. It is also possible to insert new objects at specific index points in an array object using the *insertObject* instance method. This method accepts as arguments the object to be inserted and the index position at which the insertion is to take place:

```
NSMutableArray *myColors;
int i;
```

```
int count;

NSMutableArray *myColors = [@[@"Red", @"Green", @"Blue", @"Yellow"]
mutableCopy];

[myColors insertObject: @"Indigo" atIndex: 1];
[myColors insertObject: @"Violet" atIndex: 3];

count = myColors.count;

for (i = 0; i < count; i++)
        NSLog (@"Element %i = %@", i, [myColors objectAtIndex: i]);
```

When we compile and run the code, the following output confirms that the new objects were indeed inserted at the specified index positions:

```
Element 0 = Red
Element 1 = Indigo
Element 2 = Green
Element 3 = Violet
Element 4 = Blue
Element 5 = Yellow
```

25.10 Deleting Elements from an Array Object

The NSMutableArray class provides a number of instance methods designed specifically to remove one or more elements from an array object. A sample of some of the more commonly used methods is provided below. This list is not exhaustive so refer to the Foundation Framework documentation for the NSMutableArray class for a full listing.

To remove an element at a specific index location, use the *removeObjectAtIndex* method:

```
[myColors removeObjectAtIndex: 0];
```

To remove the first instance of a specific object from an array use *removeObject*:

```
[myColors removeObject: @"Red"];
```

To remove all instances of a specific object in an array, use *removeObjectIdenticalTo*:

```
[myColors removeObjectIdenticalTo: @"Red"];
```

To remove all objects from an array, use *removeAllObjects*:

```
[myColors removeAllObjects];
```

To remove the last object in the array, use the *removeLastObject* method:

```
[myColors removeLastObject];
```

25.11 **Sorting Array Objects**

The Foundation Framework NSArray class, and the subclasses thereof, provide a number of mechanisms for sorting the elements of an array into a specific order. The simplest way to achieve this is to use the *sortedArrayUsingSelector* instance method. For example, to perform a sort on our example array using this method, we could use the following code:

```
NSArray *sortedArray;

sortedArray = [myColors

sortedArrayUsingSelector:@selector(localizedCaseInsensitiveCompare:)]
;
```

As we can see from the above example, the method returns a new array containing the elements of the original array sorted using the *localizedCaseInsensitiveCompare* method. In practice any method can be used in this context as long as that method is able to compare two objects and return an *NSOrderedAscending*, *NSOrderedSame* or *NSOrderedDescending* result.

25.12 **Summary**

NSArray is a container class designed to hold and manage a collection of objects. The class includes a set of methods that can be used to add, delete, insert and sort array elements. The elements within an array may be of any object type and, unlike some other programming languages, a single Objective-C array can contain any mix of object types.

Chapter 26

26. Objective-C Dictionary Objects

Objective-C Dictionary Object classes allow data to be stored and managed in the form of key-value pairs where both the key and the value are objects. In this chapter of *Objective-C 2.0 Essentials* we will look at how to create, initialize and work with dictionary objects in Objective-C.

26.1 What are Dictionary Objects?

In the previous chapter we looked at using array objects to store collections of objects. Dictionary objects fulfill a similar purpose except each object stored in the dictionary has associated with it a unique key (to be precise, the key is unique to the particular dictionary object). The unique key can be of any object type though to be useful they are typically string objects.

Objective-C dictionary objects are created using the *NSDictionary* and *NSMutableDictionary* classes. NSDictionary based objects are immutable (in other words once they have been created and initialized their contents cannot be modified). Mutable dictionaries are instantiated from the NSMutableDictionary class and may be modified after creation and initialization.

26.2 Creating Dictionary Objects using Methods

An empty, immutable dictionary object may be created as follows:

```
NSDictionary *bookListing = [NSDictionary dictionary];
```

Similarly, an empty mutable dictionary may be created as follows:

```
NSMutableDictionary *bookListing = [NSMutableDictionary dictionary];
```

26.3 **Initializing and Adding Entries to a Dictionary Object**

Each key-value pair contained within a dictionary is referred to as an entry. Once a relationship between a key and a value has been established that relationship cannot subsequently be modified.

New entries are added to a dictionary using the *setObject* instance method. This method takes as its arguments an object and a corresponding key:

```
NSMutableDictionary *bookListing = [NSMutableDictionary dictionary];

[bookListing setObject: @"Wind in the Willows"  forKey: @"100-
432112"];

[bookListing setObject: @"Tale of Two Cities " forKey:  @"200-
532874"];

[bookListing setObject: @"Sense and Sensibility" forKey:  @"202-
546549"];

[bookListing setObject: @"Shutter Island" forKey: @"104-109834"];
```

In the above example, the bookListing dictionary is initialized with four book names with corresponding reference codes to act as keys.

It is also possible to create and initialize a dictionary with multiple key-value pairs using the *dictionaryWithObjectsAndKeys* class method. For example, an alternative to the above code is as follows:

```
NSDictionary *bookListing = [NSDictionary
dictionaryWithObjectsAndKeys: @"Wind in the Willows", @"100-432112",
@"Tale of Two Cities ", @"200-532874",
@"Sense and Sensibility", @"202-546549",
@"Shutter Island", @"104-109834",
nil];
```

Dictionaries may also be initialized using keys and values contained in arrays using the *arrayWithObjects* method:

```
NSArray *objectsArray = @[@"Wind in the Willows", @"Tale of Two
Cities ", @"Sense and Sensibility", @"Shutter Island"];
```

```
NSArray *keysArray = @[@"100-432112", @"200-532874", @"202-546549",
@"104-109834"];


NSDictionary *bookListing = [[NSDictionary alloc] initWithObjects:
objectsArray forKeys: keysArray];
```

26.4 Initializing Dictionaries using Literal Syntax

An alternative to using methods to initialize dictionary entries involves the use of NSDictionary literals, the syntax for which is as follows:

```
NSDictionary *bookListing = @{key1 : object1, key2 : object2, key3 :
object3};
```

The code to create the example bookListing dictionary would, therefore, be written as follows using literal syntax:

```
NSDictionary *bookListing = @{ @"100-432112" : @"Wind in the
Willows",
          @"200-532874" : @"Tale of Two Cities",
          @"202-546549" : @"Sense and Sensibility",
           @"104-109834" : @"Shutter Island" };
```

Note also that the dictionary entries do not need to be terminated with a *nil* value when using literal syntax.

When using literal syntax, the initialized dictionary is, by default, immutable. In order to create a mutable dictionary object the *mutableCopy* method of the dictionary object must be called. The following code listing, for example, creates a mutable version of the bookListing dictionary:

```
NSMutableDictionary *bookListing =
                    [ @{ @"100-432112" : @"Wind in the Willows",
                    @"200-532874" : @"Tale of Two Cities",
                    @"202-546549" : @"Sense and Sensibility",
                    @"104-109834" : @"Shutter Island" }
mutableCopy];
```

26.5 **Getting an Entry Count**

A count of the number of entries in a dictionary can be obtained using the *count* instance method:

```
NSMutableDictionary *bookListing = [NSMutableDictionary dictionary];

int count;

[bookListing setObject: @"Wind in the Willows"  forKey: @"100-
432112"];
[bookListing setObject: @"Tale of Two Cities " forKey:  @"200-
532874"];
[bookListing setObject: @"Sense and Sensibility" forKey:  @"202-
546549"];
[bookListing setObject: @"Shutter Island" forKey: @"104-109834"];

NSLog (@"Number of books in dictionary = %lu", [bookListing count]);
```

26.6 **Accessing Dictionary Entries**

Dictionary entries may be accessed using either the *objectForKey:* method or a process referred to as *keyed subscripting*.

When using the *objectForKey:* method, dictionary entries are accessed by referencing the key corresponding to the required entry, for example:

```
NSLog ( @"100-432112 = %@", [bookListing objectForKey: @"100-
432112"]);
NSLog ( @"200-532874 = %@", [bookListing objectForKey: @"200-
532874"]);
NSLog ( @"202-546549 = %@", [bookListing objectForKey: @"202-
546549"]);
NSLog ( @"104-109834 = %@", [bookListing objectForKey: @"104-
109834"]);
```

When combined with the previous code and executed, we would expect to see the following output:

```
100-432112 = Wind in the Willows
200-532874 = Tale of Two Cities
202-546549 = Sense and Sensibility
104-109834 = Shutter Island
```

Alternatively, *keyed subscripting* can be used, whereby the key can be placed within square brackets. The following line of code extracts the object associated with the key 100-432112 and assigns it to an NSString object:

```
NSString *bookTitle = bookListing[@"100-432112"];
```

The current object assigned to a specific key may also be replaced by a new object using keyed subscripting. The following example code changes the book title associated with the 202-546549 key to a new title string:

```
bookListing[@"202-546549"] = @"Robinson Crusoe";
```

Keep in mind when using this syntax that the dictionary object must be initialized as being mutable in order for changes to be made to the stored objects.

26.7 **Removing Entries from a Dictionary Object**

Specific dictionary entries may be removed by referencing the key as an argument to the *removeObjectForKey* method. For example, to remove the book entry for "Shutter Island" we would write the following code:

```
[bookListing removeObjectForKey: @"104-109834"];
```

All entries in a dictionary may be removed using the *removeAllObjects* instance method:

```
[bookListing removeAllObjects];
```

26.8 **Summary**

The NSDictionary class of the Objective-C Foundation Framework is provided specifically for creating collections of objects stored as key/value pairs. Each object stored in a dictionary has associated with it a key object via which the corresponding object may be extracted, deleted or replaced.

27. Working with Directories in Objective-C

A key element of gaining proficiency in any programming language involves the ability to work with files and file systems. The level of difficulty in working with files varies from very easy to hard, depending on the programming language concerned. The C programming language, on which Objective-C is based, tended to make file handling a little hard relative to the standards of today's programmer friendly object oriented languages. The good news for Objective-C developers is that the Foundation Framework includes a number of classes designed specifically to make the task of working with files and directories as straightforward as possible.

In this chapter we will look at these classes and provide examples of how to use them to perform some basic directory operations from within an Objective-C program. In *Working with Files in Objective-C* we will take a close look at working with files using these classes.

27.1 The Objective-C NSFileManager, NSFileHandle and NSData Classes

The Foundation Framework provides three classes that are indispensable when it comes to working with files and directories:

- **NSFileManager** - The *NSFileManager* class can be used to perform basic file and directory operations such as creating, moving, reading and writing files and reading and setting file attributes. In addition, this class provides methods for, amongst other tasks, identifying the current working directory, changing to a new directory, creating directories and listing the contents of a directory.

- **NSFileHandle** - The *NSFileHandle* class is provided for performing lower level operations on files, such as seeking to a specific position in a file and reading and writing a file's contents by a specified number of byte chunks and appending data to an existing file.

- **NSData** - The *NSData* class provides a useful storage buffer into which the contents of a file may be read, or from which data may be written to a file.

27.2 **Understanding Pathnames in Objective-C**

When using the above classes, pathnames are defined using the UNIX convention. As such each component of a path is separated by a forward slash (/). Paths that do not begin with a slash are interpreted to be relative to a current working directory. For example, if the current working directory is */home/objc* and the path name is *myapp/example.m* then the file is considered to have a full pathname of */home/objc/myapp/example.m*.

In addition, the home directory of the current user can be represented using the tilde (~) character. For example the pathname *~/example.m* references a file named *example.m* located in the home directory of the current user. The home directory of another user may be referenced by prefixing the user name with a ~. For example, *~john/demo.m* references a file located in the home directory of a user named *john*.

27.3 **Obtaining a Reference to the Default NSFileManager Object**

The NSFileManager class contains a class method named *defaultManager* that is used to obtain a reference to the application's default file manager instance:

```
NSFileManager *filemgr;
filemgr = [NSFileManager defaultManager];
```

In the above example we have declared a variable named *filemgr* to point to an object of type NSFileManager, and then requested a pointer to the application's file manager and assigned it to the variable. Having obtained the object reference we can begin to use it to work with files and directories.

27.4 **Identifying the Current Working Directory**

The current working directory may be identified using the *currentDirectoryPath* instance method of our NSFileManager object. The current path is returned from the method in the form of an NSString object:

```
NSFileManager *filemgr;
NSString *currentpath;

filemgr = [NSFileManager defaultManager];
```

```
currentpath = [filemgr currentDirectoryPath];

NSLog (@"Current directory is %@", currentpath);
```

27.5 Changing to a Different Directory

The current working directory of a running Objective-C program can be changed with a call to the *changeCurrentDirectoryPath* method. The destination directory path is passed as an argument to the instance method in the form of an NSString object. Note that this method returns a boolean *YES* or *NO* result to indicate if the requested directory change was successful or not:

```
NSFileManager *filemgr;
NSString *currentpath;

filemgr = [NSFileManager defaultManager];

currentpath = [filemgr currentDirectoryPath];

NSLog (@"Current directory is %@", currentpath);

if ([filemgr changeCurrentDirectoryPath: @"/tmp/mydir"] == NO)
        NSLog (@"Cannot change directory.");

currentpath = [filemgr currentDirectoryPath];

NSLog (@"Current directory is %@", currentpath);
```

27.6 Creating a New Directory

A new directory is created using the *createDirectoryAtURL* instance method, this time passing through the pathname of the new directory as an argument in the form of an NSURL object. This method also takes additional arguments in the form of a set of attributes for the new directory and a Boolean value indicating whether or not intermediate directories should be created if they do not already exist. Specifying *nil* will use the default attributes:

```
NSFileManager *filemgr;


filemgr = [NSFileManager defaultManager];
NSURL *newDir = [NSURL fileURLWithPath:@"/tmp/mynewdir"];
[filemgr createDirectoryAtURL: newDir withIntermediateDirectories:YES
attributes: nil error:nil];
```

The *createDirectoryAtURL* method returns a Boolean result indicating the success or otherwise of the operation.

27.7 **Deleting a Directory**

An existing directory may be removed from the file system using the *removeItemAtPath* method, passing through the path of the directory to be removed as an argument:

```
NSFileManager *filemgr;


filemgr = [NSFileManager defaultManager];
[filemgr removeItemAtPath: @"/tmp/mynewdir" error: nil];
```

27.8 **Renaming or Moving a File or Directory**

An existing file or directory may be moved (also known as renaming) using the *moveItemAtURL* method. This method takes the source and destination pathnames as arguments in the form of NSURL objects and requires that the destination path not already exist. If the target exists, a boolean NO result is returned by the method to indicate failure of the operation:

```
NSFileManager *filemgr;


filemgr = [NSFileManager defaultManager];


NSURL *oldDir = [NSURL fileURLWithPath:@"/tmp/mynewdir"];
NSURL *newDir = [NSURL fileURLWithPath:@"/tmp/mynewdir2"];


[filemgr moveItemAtURL: oldDir toURL: newDir error: nil];
```

27.9 **Getting a Directory File Listing**

A listing of the files contained within a specified directory can be obtained using the *contentsOfDirectoryAtPath* method. This method takes the directory pathname as an argument and returns an *NSArray* object containing the names of the files and subdirectories in that directory:

```
NSFileManager *filemgr;
NSString *currentpath;
NSArray *filelist;
int count;
int i;

filemgr = [NSFileManager defaultManager];

filelist = [filemgr contentsOfDirectoryAtPath: @"/tmp" error: nil];

count = [filelist count];

for (i = 0; i < count; i++)
        NSLog (@"%@", [filelist objectAtIndex: i]);
```

When executed as part of a program, the above code excerpt will display a listing of all the files located in the */tmp* directory.

27.10 **Getting the Attributes of a File or Directory**

The attributes of a file or directory can be obtained using the *attributesOfItemAtPath* method. This takes as arguments the path of the directory and an optional NSError object into which information about any errors will be placed (may be specified as NULL if this information is not required). The results are returned in the form of an *NSDictionary* dictionary object (for details of working with dictionary objects refer to *Objective-C Dictionary Objects*). The keys for this dictionary are as follows:

```
NSFileType
NSFileTypeDirectory
NSFileTypeRegular
NSFileTypeSymbolicLink
```

```
NSFileTypeSocket
NSFileTypeCharacterSpecial
NSFileTypeBlockSpecial
NSFileTypeUnknown
NSFileSize
NSFileModificationDate
NSFileReferenceCount
NSFileDeviceIdentifier
NSFileOwnerAccountName
NSFileGroupOwnerAccountName
NSFilePosixPermissions
NSFileSystemNumber
NSFileSystemFileNumber
NSFileExtensionHidden
NSFileHFSCreatorCode
NSFileHFSTypeCode
NSFileImmutable
NSFileAppendOnly
NSFileCreationDate
NSFileOwnerAccountID
NSFileGroupOwnerAccountID
```

For example, we can extract the creation date, file type and POSIX permissions for the *tmp* directory using the following code excerpt:

```
NSFileManager *filemgr;
NSDictionary *attribs;


filemgr = [NSFileManager defaultManager];


attribs = [filemgr attributesOfItemAtPath: @"/tmp" error: NULL];


NSLog (@"Created on %@", [attribs objectForKey: NSFileCreationDate]);
NSLog (@"File type %@", [attribs objectForKey: NSFileType]);
NSLog (@"POSIX Permissions %@", [attribs objectForKey:
NSFilePosixPermissions]);
```

When executed on a Mac OS X system, we can expect to see the following output (note that *tmp* on a Mac OS X system is a symbolic link to *private/tmp*):

```
Created on 2012-01-14 07:34:32 -0500
File type NSFileTypeSymbolicLink
POSIX Permissions 493
```

27.11 **Summary**

Regardless of whether you plan to develop Objective-C applications for Mac OS X or iOS, it is inevitable that at some point it will be necessary to interact with the file system to store data. Fortunately, Objective-C provides a range of classes that make it easy to work with and navigate the file system directory structure. Having covered the basics of directory handling in Objective-C in this chapter, the next chapter will focus on working specifically with files.

28. Working with Files in Objective-C

In *Working with Directories in Objective-C* we looked at the NSFileManager, NSFileHandle and NSData Foundation Framework classes and discussed how the NSFileManager class in particular enables us to work with directories in Objective-C. In this chapter we move on from working with directories to covering the details of working with files using all three of these classes.

28.1 Getting the NSFileManager Reference

First we need to recap the steps necessary to obtain a reference to an instance of the NSFileManager class. As discussed in the previous chapter, the NSFileManager class contains a class method named *defaultManager* that is used to obtain a reference to the NSFileManager object instance:

```
NSFileManager *filemgr;
filemgr = [NSFileManager defaultManager];
```

28.2 Checking if a File Exists

The NSFileManager class contains an instance method named *fileExistsAtPath* that checks whether a specified file already exists. The method takes as an argument an NSString object containing the path to the file and returns a boolean YES or NO value indicating the presence or otherwise of that file:

```
NSFileManager *filemgr;

filemgr = [NSFileManager defaultManager];

if ([filemgr fileExistsAtPath: @"/tmp/myfile.txt" ] == YES)
        NSLog (@"File exists");
else
```

```
NSLog (@"File not found");
```

28.3 Comparing the Contents of Two Files

The contents of two files can be compared for equality using the *contentsEqualAtPath* method. This method takes as arguments the paths to the two files to be compared and returns a boolean YES or NO to indicate whether the file contents match:

```
NSFileManager *filemgr;

filemgr = [NSFileManager defaultManager];

if ([filemgr contentsEqualAtPath: @"/tmp/myfile.txt" andPath:
@"/tmp/sales.txt"] == YES)
        NSLog (@"File contents match");
else
        NSLog (@"File contents do not match");
```

28.4 Checking if a File is Readable/Writable/Executable/Deletable

Most operating systems provide some level of file access control. These typically take the form of attributes that control the level of access to a file for each user or user group. As such, it is not a certainty that your program will have read or write access to a particular file, or the appropriate permissions to delete or execute it. The quickest way to find out if your program has a particular access permission is to use the *isReadableFileAtPath*, *isWritableFileAtPath*, *isExecutableFileAtPath* and *isDeletableFileAtPath* methods. Each method takes a single argument in the form of the path to the file to be checked and returns a boolean YES or NO result. For example, the following code excerpt checks to find out if a file is writable:

```
NSFileManager *filemgr;

filemgr = [NSFileManager defaultManager];

if ([filemgr isWritableFileAtPath: @"/tmp/myfile.txt"]  == YES)
        NSLog (@"File is writable");
else
```

```
    NSLog (@"File is read only");
```

To check for other access permissions simply substitute the corresponding method name in place of *isWritableFileAtPath* in the above example.

28.5 Moving/Renaming a File

A file may be renamed (assuming adequate permissions) using the *moveItemAtURL* method. This method returns a boolean YES or NO result and takes as arguments the pathname for the file to be moved, the destination path and an optional NSError object into which information describing any errors encountered during the operation will be placed. If no error description information is required, this argument may be set to nil. Note that if the destination file path already exists this operation will fail.

```
NSFileManager *filemgr;

filemgr = [NSFileManager defaultManager];

NSURL *oldPath = [NSURL fileURLWithPath:@"/tmp/myfile.txt"];
NSURL *newPath= [NSURL fileURLWithPath:@"/tmp/newfile.txt"];

[filemgr moveItemAtURL: oldPath toURL: newPath error: nil];
```

28.6 Copying a File

File copying can be achieved using the *copyItemAtPath* method. As with the *move* method, this takes as arguments the source and destination pathnames and an optional NSError object. Success of the operation is indicated by the returned boolean value:

```
NSFileManager *filemgr;

filemgr = [NSFileManager defaultManager];

if ([filemgr copyItemAtPath: @"/tmp/myfile.txt" toPath:
@"/Users/demo/newfile.txt" error: nil]   == YES)
        NSLog (@"Copy successful");
else
```

```
        NSLog (@"Copy failed");
```

28.7 **Removing a File**

The *removeItemAtPath* method removes the specified file from the file system. The method takes as arguments the pathname of the file to be removed and an optional NSError object. The success of the operation is, as usual, reported in the form of a boolean YES or NO return value:

```
NSFileManager *filemgr;

filemgr = [NSFileManager defaultManager];

if ([filemgr removeItemAtPath: @"/tmp/myfile.txt" error: NULL]  ==
YES)
        NSLog (@"Remove successful");
else
        NSLog (@"Remove failed");
```

28.8 **Creating a Symbolic Link**

A symbolic link to a particular file may be created using the *createSymbolicLinkAtPath* method. This takes as arguments the path of the symbolic link, the path to the file to which the link is to refer and an optional NSError object. For example, the following code creates a symbolic link from */tmp/myfile2.txt* that links to the pre-existing file */tmp/myfile.txt*:

```
NSFileManager *filemgr;

filemgr = [NSFileManager defaultManager];

if ([filemgr createSymbolicLinkAtPath: @"/tmp/myfile2.txt"
                withDestinationPath: @"/tmp/myfile.txt" error: nil]
== YES)
        NSLog (@"Link successful");
else
        NSLog (@"Link failed");
```

28.9 **Reading and Writing Files with NSFileManager**

The NSFileManager class includes some basic file reading and writing capabilities. These capabilities are somewhat limited when compared to the options provided by the NSFileHandle class, but can be useful nonetheless.

Firstly, the contents of a file may be read and stored in an NSData object through the use of the *contentsAtPath* method:

```
NSFileManager *filemgr;
NSData *databuffer;

filemgr = [NSFileManager defaultManager];

databuffer = [filemgr contentsAtPath: @"/tmp/myfile.txt" ];
```

Having stored the contents of a file in an NSData object, that data may subsequently be written out to a new file using the *createFileAtPath* method:

```
databuffer = [filemgr contentsAtPath: @"/tmp/myfile.txt" ];

[filemgr createFileAtPath: @"/tmp/newfile.txt" contents: databuffer
attributes: nil];
```

In the above example we have essentially copied the contents from an existing file to a new file. This, however, gives us no control over how much data is to be read or written and does not allow us to append data to the end of an existing file. If the file */tmp/newfile.txt* in the above example had already existed it, and any data it contained, would have been overwritten by the contents of the source file. Clearly some more flexible mechanism is required. This is provided by the Foundation Framework in the form of the *NSFileHandle* class.

28.10 **Working with Files using the NSFileHandle Class**

The NSFileHandle class provides a range of methods designed to provide a more advanced mechanism for working with files. In addition to files, this class can also be used for working with devices and network sockets. In the following sections we will look at some of the more common uses for this class.

28.11 **Creating an NSFileHandle Object**

An NSFileHandle object can be created when opening a file for reading, writing or updating (reading and writing). This is achieved using the *fileHandleForReadingAtPath*, *fileHandleForWritingAtPath* and *fileHandleForUpdatingAtPath* methods respectively. Having opened a file, it must subsequently be closed when we have finished working with it using the *closeFile* method. If an attempt to open a file fails, for example because an attempt is made to open a non-existent file for reading, these methods return *nil*.

For example, the following code excerpt opens a file for reading and writing and then closes it without actually doing anything to the file:

```
NSFileHandle *file;

file = [NSFileHandle fileHandleForWritingAtPath: @"/tmp/myfile.txt"];

if (file == nil)
        NSLog(@"Failed to open file");

[file closeFile];
```

28.12 **NSFileHandle File Offsets and Seeking**

NSFileHandle objects maintain a pointer to the current position in a file. This is referred to as the *offset*. When a file is first opened the offset is set to 0 (the beginning of the file). This means that any read or write operations we perform using the NSFileHandle methods will take place at offset 0 in the file. To perform operations at different locations in a file (for example to append data to the end of the file) it is first necessary to *seek* to the required offset. For example to move the current offset to the end of the file, use the *seekToEndOfFile* method. Alternatively, *seekToFileOffset* allows you to specify the precise location in the file to which the offset is to be positioned. Finally, the current offset may be identified using the *offsetInFile* method. In order to accommodate large files, the offset is stored in the form of an unsigned long long.

The following example opens a file for reading and then performs a number of method calls to move the offset to different positions, outputting the current offset after each move:

```
NSFileHandle *file;


file = [NSFileHandle fileHandleForUpdatingAtPath:
@"/tmp/myfile.txt"];


if (file == nil)
        NSLog(@"Failed to open file");


NSLog (@"Offset = %llu", [file offsetInFile]);


[file seekToEndOfFile];


NSLog (@"Offset = %llu", [file offsetInFile]);


[file seekToFileOffset: 30];


NSLog (@"Offset = %llu", [file offsetInFile]);


[file closeFile];
```

File offsets are a key aspect of working with files using the NSFileHandle class so it is worth taking extra time to make sure you understand the concept. Without knowing where the current offset is in a file it is impossible to know where in the file data will be read or written.

28.13 Reading Data from a File

Once a file has been opened and assigned a file handle, the contents of that file may be read from the current offset position. The *readDataOfLength* method reads a specified number of bytes of data from the file starting at the current offset. For example, the following code reads 5 bytes of data from offset 10 in a file. The data read is returned encapsulated in an NSData object:

```
NSFileHandle *file;
NSData *databuffer;


file = [NSFileHandle fileHandleForReadingAtPath: @"/tmp/myfile.txt"];
```

```
if (file == nil)
        NSLog(@"Failed to open file");


[file seekToFileOffset: 10];


databuffer = [file readDataOfLength: 5];


[file closeFile];
```

Alternatively, the *readDataToEndOfFile* method will read all the data in the file starting at the current offset and ending at the end of the file.

28.14 **Writing Data to a File**

The *writeData* method writes the data contained in an NSData object to the file starting at the location of the offset. Note that this does not insert data but rather overwrites any existing data in the file at the corresponding location.

To see this in action we need to begin with a file. Using a text editor, create a file named quickfox.txt, enter the following text and save it in the /tmp directory:

```
The quick brown fox jumped over the lazy dog
```

Next, we will write a program that opens the file for updating, seeks to position 10 and then writes some data at that location:

```
#import <Foundation/Foundation.h>

int main (int argc, const char * argv[])
{
    @autoreleasepool {

        NSFileHandle *file;
        NSMutableData *data;

        const char *bytestring = "black dog";
```

```
        data = [NSMutableData dataWithBytes:bytestring
length:strlen(bytestring)];
        file = [NSFileHandle fileHandleForUpdatingAtPath:
@"/tmp/quickfox.txt"];


        if (file == nil)
                NSLog(@"Failed to open file");


        [file seekToFileOffset: 10];


        [file writeData: data];


        [file closeFile];
    }
    return 0;
}
```

When the above program is compiled and executed the contents of the *quickfox.txt* will have changed to:

```
The quick black dog jumped over the lazy dog
```

28.15 **Truncating a File**

A file may be truncated at the specified offset using the *truncateFileAtOffset* method. To delete the entire contents of a file, specify an offset of 0 when calling this method:

```
NSFileHandle *file;


file = [NSFileHandle fileHandleForUpdatingAtPath:
@"/tmp/quickfox.txt"];


if (file == nil)
      NSLog(@"Failed to open file");
      [file truncateFileAtOffset: 0];
      [file closeFile];
```

28.16 **Summary**

As has come to be expected from modern object oriented programming languages, the Objective-C Foundation Framework provides a set of classes designed to make it easier to work with the file system for the purposes of locally storing user and application files and data. In this and the preceding chapter, details of file and directory handling in Objective-C have been covered in some detail.

29. Constructing and Manipulating Paths with NSPathUtilities

In this final chapter on working with files and directories in Objective-C we will be covering the utilities provided by the Foundation Framework designed to aid in the process of working with path names in a structured and platform neutral way.

29.1 The Anatomy of a Path

A path defines the location of a file in a file system. For example, a file located in the home directory of a user named John on a Mac OS X system will have the following path:

```
/Users/John/myfile.txt
```

In this example, the filename is *myfile.txt* and the rest of the path defines where in the directory structure the file is located.

The same file on a Linux system might have the following path:

```
/home/john/myfile.txt
```

Paths can also become quite convoluted. For example:

```
~demo/objc/code/../header/./mycode.h
```

The primary purpose of the *NSPathUtilities* is to make it easier to perform common tasks on a path. These utilities also provide a useful mechanism for finding a temporary directory, regardless of the platform on which an Objective-C program is running.

29.2 Finding a Temporary Directory

Most operating systems have a standard directory provided specifically for the purposes of temporarily storing files. Other systems also provide a different temporary directory for each user. The exact location differs depending on the platform in question, so in order to make your code compatible with as many platforms as possible it is unwise to make assumptions about the location of this temporary directory. Instead, it is much safer to use the *NSTemporaryDirectory()* method to identify the appropriate directory. This function returns the temporary directory for the current user in the form of an *NSString* object. The following code excerpt identifies and then displays the temporary directory using the *NSTemporaryDirectory()* function:

```
NSString *tempdir;

tempdir = NSTemporaryDirectory();
NSLog (@"Temp Dir = %@", tempdir);
```

29.3 Getting the Current User's Home Directory

The home directory of the current user can be identified using the *NSHomeDirectory()* function. This function takes no arguments and returns an NSString object containing the path to the home directory of the user executing the program:

```
NSString *homedir;

homedir = NSHomeDirectory();

NSLog (@"Home directory of current user is %@", homedir);
```

29.4 Getting the Home Directory of a Specified User

The home directory of any user on a system can be obtained using the *NSHomeDirectoryForUser()* function. This function takes as its sole argument an NSString object containing the name of the user and returns another NSString object containing the corresponding home directory:

```
NSString *homedir;
NSString *username = @"Paul";

homedir = NSHomeDirectoryForUser(username);

NSLog (@"Home directory of user %@ is %@", username, homedir);
```

If the requested user does not exist on the system the function will return *null*.

29.5 **Extracting the Filename from a Path**

As previously discussed, a path can consist of the directory in which a file is located, followed by the name of the file. A common requirement when working with files when programming in any language is to extract just the file name from a path. This can easily be achieved using the *lastPathComponent* method:

```
NSString *samplepath = @"/Users/demo/objc/sample.m";
NSString *filename;

filename = [samplepath lastPathComponent];

NSLog (@"lastPathComponent = %@", filename);
```

When executed, the above code excerpt will display the filename part of the path, i.e. *sample.m*.

29.6 **Extracting the Filename Extension**

Filenames with characters after the final '.' character are said to have a filename extension. For example, the filename extension for a file named *myfile.txt* is *txt*. The filename extension may be extracted from a path using the *pathExtension* method:

```
NSString *samplepath = @"/Users/demo/objc/sample.m";
NSString *pathext;

pathext = [samplepath pathExtension];

NSLog (@"pathExtension = %@", pathext);
```

The above code will output the filename extension for the file referenced in the samplepath string, in this case m.

29.7 **Standardizing a Path**

It is surprising how quickly a path can become complicated, especially when allowing a user to navigate through a file system. The NSUtilities package provides the *stringByStandardizingPath* method. In the following code we will use this method to make some sense out of a path that reads as follows:

```
~demo/objc/code/../header/./../includes/mycode.h
```

```
NSString *samplepath =
@"/Users/demo/objc/code/../header/./../includes/mycode.h";
NSString *cleanpath;


cleanpath = [samplepath stringByStandardizingPath];


NSLog (@"Standardized path = %@", cleanpath);
```

The output from the above code will report to us that the convoluted path resolves down to the much simpler:

```
/Users/demo/objc/includes/mycode.h
```

29.8 **Extracting the Components of a Path**

The *pathComponents* method extracts the various components that comprise a complete path and returns them in an NSArray:

```
NSString *samplepath = @"/Users/demo/objc/code/includes/mycode.h";
NSString *component;
NSArray *pathcomponents;


pathcomponents = [samplepath pathComponents];


for (component in pathcomponents)
        NSLog (@"component = %@", component);
```

When executed, the above code will produce the following output:

```
component = /
component = Users
component = demo
component = objc
```

```
component = code
component = includes
component = mycode.h
```

30. Copying Objects in Objective-C

In Pointers and Indirection in Objective-C we discussed the fact that when working with objects in Objective-C we are essentially using variables that contain pointers to the memory addresses where the objects are stored. We also mentioned the problems this presents when we want to copy an object. In this chapter of *Objective-C 2.0 Essentials* we will look at the steps necessary to copy an object.

30.1 Objects and Pointers

Before we look at copying objects we should first recap the issue of objects and indirection. When we create an object in Objective-C, we assign the object to a variable. Consider, for example, the following Objective-C code excerpt:

```
BankAccount *account1;
BankAccount *account1 = [[BankAccount alloc] init];
```

The above code creates a variable named account1 and declares it as being of type pointer to an object of type *BankAccount.* The alloc and init method calls create the object in memory and return the address of that object which is then assigned to *account1.* Clearly, therefore, *account1* is not storing the actual object but rather holding a pointer to the memory location of the object.

If we tried to copy the object using the assignment operator, therefore, all we would be doing is copying the address value from one variable to another:

```
BankAccount *account2;
account2 = account1;
```

The above code will provide us with two variables, both of which point to the same object. If we really want a separate copy of an object, therefore, we must specifically perform a copy.

30.2 **Copying an Object in Objective-C using the <NSCopying> Protocol**

In *An Overview of Objective-C Object Oriented Programming* the topic of object-oriented programming was covered. In particular the fact that most classes are derived from the *NSObject* base class was discussed. The advantage of deriving new classes from *NSObject* is that those classes inherit a number of useful methods designed specifically for creating, managing and manipulating objects. Two such methods are the *copy* and *mutableCopy* methods. These methods implement something called the *<NSCopying> Protocol*. This protocol defines what must be implemented in an object in order for it to be copyable using the *copy* and *mutableCopy* methods. Classes from the Foundation Framework will typically already be compliant with the <NSCopying> Protocol. We can, therefore, simply call the *copy* or *mutableCopy* methods to create a copy of an object:

```
NSString *myString1 = @"Hello";
NSString *myString2;


myString2 = [myString1 mutableCopy];
```

On execution of the *mutableCopy* method in the above example we will have two independent string objects both of which contain the same string. Because we used the mutable version of the copy method we will be able to modify the contents of *myString2*. In doing so, no change will occur to *myString1* because that is an entirely different object.

If we attempted to use either of these copying methods on our own classes without implementing the <NSCopying> protocol the code will fail to run. Take, for example, the BankAccount class created in *An Overview of Objective-C Object Oriented Programming*. If we were to create an instance of the class and then try to call the *copy* methods we would be presented with a runtime error similar to the following:

```
*** -[BankAccount copyWithZone:]: unrecognized selector sent to
instance 0x1034f0


*** Terminating app due to uncaught exception
'NSInvalidArgumentException', reason: '*** -[BankAccount
copyWithZone:]: unrecognized selector sent to instance 0x1034f0'
```

The reason for this error is that the *copy* and *mutableCopy* methods inherited from the *NSObject* class are trying to call a method called *copyWithZone*. Unfortunately we have not yet implemented this method in our BankAccount class. The next step, therefore, is to learn how to write such a method.

30.3 <NSCopying> Protocol and copyWithZone Method Implementation

The first step in implementing the <NSCopying> protocol is to declare that the class conforms to the protocol. This is achieved in the @interface section of the class. For example:

```
@interface BankAccount: NSObject <NSCopying>
```

Also in the implementation we need to declare that the class includes a method named *copyWithZone* that returns a new object and accepts the zone of the source object as an argument. The entire *@interface* section of our class will now read as follows:

```
@interface BankAccount: NSObject <NSCopying>
{
        double accountBalance;
        long accountNumber;
}
-(void) setAccount: (long) y andBalance: (double) x;
-(double) getAccountBalance;
-(long) getAccountNumber;
-(void) setAccountBalance: (double) x;
-(void) setAccountNumber: (long) y;
-(void) displayAccountInfo;
-(id) copyWithZone: (NSZone *) zone;
@end
```

In our @implementation section we now need to write the code for our *copyWithZone* method. This method creates a new BankAccount object, copies the values of the instance variables (in this case *accountBalance* and *accountNumber*) and returns a pointer to the new object:

```
-(id) copyWithZone: (NSZone *) zone
{
        BankAccount *accountCopy = [[BankAccount allocWithZone: zone] init];
```

```
        [accountCopy setAccount: accountNumber andBalance:
accountBalance];

        return accountCopy;

}
```

If we now bring this all together we can successfully utilize the *copy* method:

```
int main (int argc, const char * argv[])
{

    @autoreleasepool {

        BankAccount *account1;
        BankAccount *account2;


        account1 = [BankAccount alloc];


        account1 = [account1 init];


        [account1 setAccountBalance: 1500.53];
        [account1 setAccountNumber: 34543212];


        [account1 displayAccountInfo];


        account2 = [account1 copy];


        [account2 displayAccountInfo];
    }
    return 0;
}
```

Now when executed, the above code creates a copy of the object referenced by *account1* and assigns a pointer to the new object to variable *account2*.

30.4 **Performing a Deep Copy**

The copying techniques we have looked at so far in this chapter are referred to as *shallow copies*. This means that if the *copy* or *mutableCopy* methods are used to copy an object that itself contains instance variables that are themselves pointers to objects, the copy will also contain pointers to the same objects. To better understand this concept, consider an NSArray object that contains as its elements pointers to three string objects:

```
NSArray *myArray1;
NSArray *myArray2;
NSMutableString *tmpStr;
NSMutableString *string1;
NSMutableString *string2;
NSMutableString *string3;


string1 = [NSMutableString stringWithString: @"Red"];
string2 = [NSMutableString stringWithString: @"Green"];
string3 = [NSMutableString stringWithString: @"Blue"];


myArray1 = [NSMutableArray arrayWithObjects: string1, string2,
string3, nil];
```

We now have an array named *myArray1* that contains as elements three variables that each point to a string object. We could now create a copy of that array and assign it to variable pointer *myArray2*:

```
myArray2 = [myArray1 copy];
```

The *myArray2* object is a separate object, but the elements it contains still point to the same three string objects. We can prove this by modifying the string contained in element 0 of *myArray1* from "Red" to "Yellow" and then displaying the contents of the object referenced by the first element of *myArray2*:

```
tmpStr = [myArray1 objectAtIndex: 0];


[tmpStr setString: @"Yellow"];


NSLog (@"First element of myArray2 = %@", [myArray2 objectAtIndex:
0]);
```

When compiled and executed, the NSLog call will display the following output:

```
First element of myArray2 = Yellow
```

Clearly when we changed the object pointed to by element 0 of *myArray1* we were also changing the object pointed to by element 0 or *myArray2*. This proves that even though we created a copy of *myArray1* to create *myArray2* the pointers contained in the array stayed the same.

In order to create entirely new instance objects we need to perform a *deep copy*. This can be achieved by writing the object and its constituent elements to an archive and then reading it back into the new object. Our example would, therefore, be rewritten as follows:

```
NSArray *myArray1;
NSArray *myArray2;
NSMutableString *tmpStr;
NSMutableString *string1;
NSMutableString *string2;
NSMutableString *string3;
NSData *buffer;

string1 = [NSMutableString stringWithString: @"Red"];
string2 = [NSMutableString stringWithString: @"Green"];
string3 = [NSMutableString stringWithString: @"Blue"];

myArray1 = [NSMutableArray arrayWithObjects: string1, string2,
string3, nil];

buffer = [NSKeyedArchiver archivedDataWithRootObject: myArray1];
myArray2 = [NSKeyedUnarchiver unarchiveObjectWithData: buffer];

tmpStr = [myArray1 objectAtIndex: 0];

[tmpStr setString: @"Yellow"];

NSLog (@"First element of myArray1 = %@", [myArray1 objectAtIndex:
0]);
NSLog (@"First element of myArray2 = %@", [myArray2 objectAtIndex:
0]);
```

When executed, the following output will be displayed clearly indicating that the objects referenced in *myArray2* are entirely different to those referenced by *myArray1*. We have, therefore performed a deep copy.

```
First element of myArray1 = Yellow
First element of myArray2 = Red
```

31. Using Objective-C Preprocessor Directives

In general terms the compilation of Objective-C programs from source code to executable binary is a three phase process. In the first phase, a tool called the *preprocessor* scans the human written source code and converts it to compiler friendly content and format. In the second phase the compiler generates object code (usually in the form of a file with a .o filename extension) from the preprocessed source code. Finally, the linker brings all the object code modules and libraries together, resolves symbol references and creates the executable binary.

The preprocessor phase also searches for special *directives* written by the programmer and converts them to code that can be handled by the compiler. Each directive begins with a hash (#) character, and serves to make the Objective-C programming task easier and code easier to read and manage. In this chapter of *Objective-C 2.0 Essentials* we will look at some of these preprocessor directives.

31.1 The #define Statement

The #define statement can be used for a variety of purposes and is probably the most flexible of preprocessor directives. Perhaps one of the most common uses is to give frequently used constant values in a program a programmer friendly name and single point of definition. For the sake of an example, let's say you need to frequently use the boiling temperature of water (a point of contention but for the purposes of this example we will assume it to be 99.61 degrees Celsius) throughout your Objective-C program. One option might be to simply enter the constant value wherever it is needed. For example:

```
double liquidTemp = 99.61 - ambientTemp;
```

The above code works but doesn't do much to explain why the number 99.61 is used. Another problem with this approach is that if one day the program needs to be modified to use a different temperature for the boiling point of water (like I said, this is a point of contention) you will have to change every instance of 99.61 in your code, while making sure you don't also change any instances of 99.61 that aren't related to the boiling point of water.

A much better approach is to assign the value a human friendly name using the #define directive:

```
#define BOILTEMP 99.61
```

Now, whenever the boiling point is needed in the code it can be referenced by the defined name instead of the constant value:

```
double liquidTemp = BOILTEMP - ambientTemp;
```

Now when we look at the code we can ascertain what is happening simply because the constant now has a meaningful name. In addition, if we ever need to specify a different temperature we just change the #define value and the change will be picked up by all references to the definition.

A #define directive can also contain an expression. A somewhat contrived example being:

```
#define TWOBYTWO 2 * 2
```

This can then be referenced in code. Continuing with our example, the following code will output "The result is 4":

```
NSLog (@"Result is %i", TWOBYTWO);
```

31.2 Creating Macros with the #define Statement

The #define statement may also be used in a more advanced fashion to create small fragments of code called *macros*. These can be thought of as small functions that can accept arguments, perform operations and return results. The following definition declares a macro designed to multiply two numbers together:

```
#define CalcInterest(x,y) ( x * y )
```

Having declared the macro, we can now call it from the code:

```
int earnings = CalcInterest(10,5));
```

31.3 Changing the Objective-C Language with #define

My first ever job involved writing communications software using the C programming language (on which Objective-C is based). I inherited some code written by a former employee who loathed the C language and preferred to use another programming language (the name of which escapes me). When I looked at his C code it looked nothing like any C code I had ever seen before in my life. After about an hour of trying to understand how this could be possible (surely the compiler should have refused to compile this) I realized the other programmer had used the #define compiler directive to "modify" the syntax of the C programming language to make it look more like his preferred language. Whilst I am not suggesting that you too go to these lengths it is worth knowing that such adaptability is provided by the #define preprocessor statement.

Let's begin with a simple example and write a definition that assigns the word *MINUS* to the minus sign (-):

```
#define MINUS -
```

Having done this, we can now perform subtractions by using the word *MINUS*:

```
int result;

result = 20 MINUS 10;

NSLog (@"Result = %i", result);
```

Now suppose that you, rather like the programmer whose code I inherited, dislike the curly braces ({}) used to encapsulate code blocks on Objective-C. You could, if you were so inclined, declare the words *Begin* and *End* to represent the open and close braces as follows:

```
#define Begin {
#define End }
```

Having done this, you would then be able to write code that looks like this (and still have it compile):

```
#import <Foundation/Foundation.h>


#define Begin {
#define End }

int main (int argc, const char * argv[])
Begin
    @autoreleasepool Begin

        int i;
        int j = 10;

        for (i=0; i<10; i++)
        Begin
                j += i;
                NSLog (@"j = %i", j);
        End
    End
    return 0;
End
```

31.4 **Undefining a Definition with #undef**

To undefine a definition made previously in a source file, use the *#undef* statement:

```
#define INTEL_X86


// .... Objective-C code

#undef INTEL_X86

// ... more code
```

31.5 **Conditional Compilation**

The preprocessor supports a range of statements designed for the purposes of defining areas of code that should or should not be compiled depending on a particular setting. This is of particular importance when you have a range of code statements that are to be run when you compile your code in a debug mode.

Suppose, for example, that in debug mode you have written a number of calls to NSLog to output diagnostic information. These would be encapsulated in *ifdef* / *endif* statements as follows:

```
#ifdef DEBUG
    NSLog (@"File search complete. Found %i files", filecount");
#endif
```

Under normal conditions this *ifdef* construct will prevent the NSLog line from being compiled. In order to enable debugging code, DEBUG must be defined. This can either be achieved in the code by adding the following line:

```
#define DEBUG
```

or at the command-line when compiling the program:

```
clang -objc-arc -framework Foundation -D DEBUG myapp.m -o myapp
```

Conditional compilation is also invaluable when writing code that needs to compile on more than one platform. In this situation it is likely that the *ifdef* / *else* / *endif* construct will be needed:

```
#ifdef INTEL_X86

// ... 32-bit specific code here

#else

// ... 64-bit specific code here

#endif
```

Similarly, the *ifndef* statement can be used to define code to be compiled when something is not defined:

```
#ifndef INTEL_X86

// .. 64-bit code here ...

#endif
```

31.6 The #import Directive

The final directive we will look at is one you will probably have seen many times already in previous chapters. The *#import* directive allows you to import include files into your source files. We have done this many times when we have included the Foundation Framework headers in our example programs:

```
#import <Foundation/Foundation.h>
```

This particular import statement has the path encapsulated by < and > characters. This means that the specified header file is to be found relative to the system includes directory (or any other include directories defined for the compilation). To import a header file relative to the directory containing the source file, the file name must enclosed in quotes:

```
#import "includes/myincludes.h"
```

The above example imports a header file named *myincludes.h* located in a sub-directory of the current directory called *includes*. This technique may also be used to specify an absolute path (i.e. one that is not relative to the current directory):

```
#import "/Users/demo/objc/includes/myincludes.h"
```

As you develop larger and more complex applications you will, of course, be writing and importing many of your own header files. Many of these will contain the preprocessor directives we have covered in this chapter.

Index

#

#define, 207
#endif, 211
#ifdef, 211
#import, 212
#undef, 210

@

@implementation, 76
@interface, 76
@private, 74
@property, 89, 90
@protected, 74
@public, 74

<

<NSCopying> Protocol, 200

A

alloc, 77, 83
AND (&&) operator, 32
ARC, 10, 14
argc, 125
arguments, 73
argv, 125
Arithmetic Operators, 28
Array
    number of elements, 163
Array Objects, 161
Arrays
    adding elements, 165
    deleting elements, 166
    immutable, 161
    mutable, 161
    sorting, 167
assignment operator, 23
Associativity, 40
auto, 121
Automatic Reference Counting, 10, 14

B

base class, 95
binary operators, 28, 31
Bitwise AND, 34
Bitwise Left Shift, 36
Bitwise Operators, 33
Bitwise OR, 35
Bitwise Right Shift, 36
Bitwise XOR, 35
Block Scope, 113
BOOL, 19
Boolean Logical Operators, 31
break statement, 53, 61, 66
Build Phases, 11
Build Rules, 11

C

C programming language, 3
case statement, 53
char, 17, 141
child class, 95
clang
    compiler, 14
clang compiler front end, 14
class hierarchy, 95
Class Implementation, 76
Class Interface, 70
class methods, 73

Index

Index

CPSIA information can be obtained at www.ICGtesting.com
Printed in the USA
LVOW03s2140100814

398499LV00005B/62/P